1973

$\mathcal{L} u a$
apr
73

This book may be kept

The New Schools

Series editor: Paulhans Peters

Design & Planning

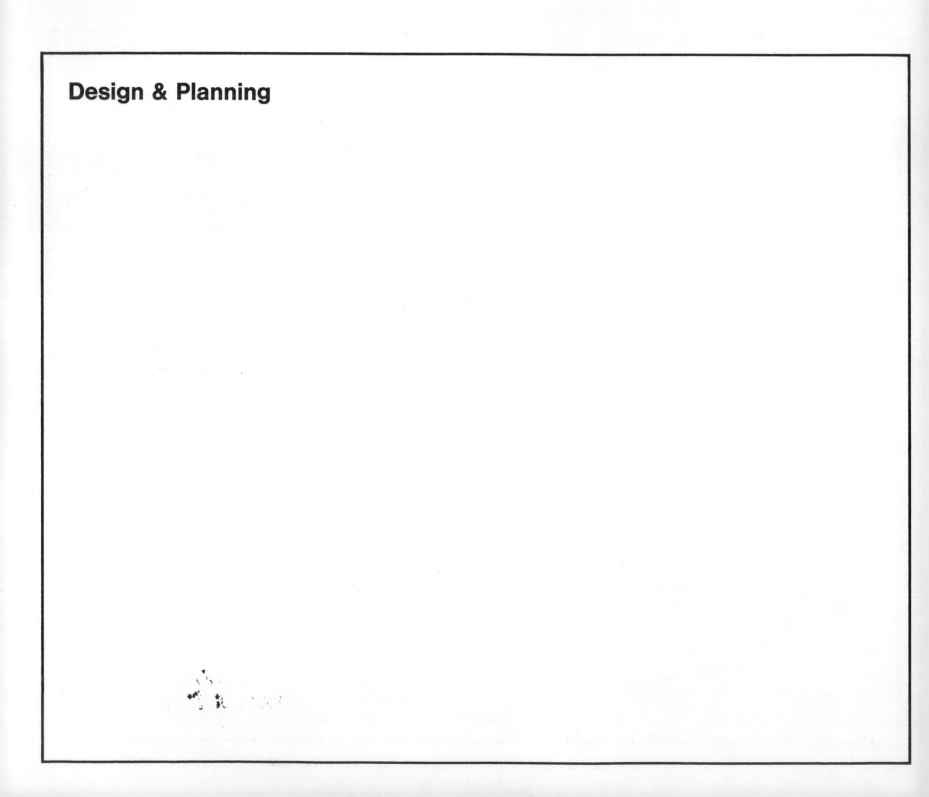

James J. Morisseau

The New Schools

VNR **Van Nostrand Reinhold Company / New York**

Van Nostrand Reinhold Company Regional Offices:
New York Cincinnati Chicago Millbrae Dallas
Van Nostrand Reinhold Company International Offices:
London Toronto Melbourne

Published by Van Nostrand Reinhold Company, 450 West 33rd Street,
New York, N.Y. 10001.
Published simultaneously in Canada by Van Nostrand Reinhold Ltd.

16 15 14 13 12 11 10 9 8 7 6 5 4 3 2

Contents

Introduction

School architecture is undergoing a transformation. The resulting new look in schoolhouse design is most evident today in the United States and Canada, but there are indications, particularly in Australia and Western Europe, that the rest of the world soon may follow suit.

Not too many years ago, the planning of a school was a relatively straightforward, uncomplicated process. The architect simply was told to provide a given number of classrooms of a fixed pupil capacity. The classrooms had to meet state-mandated standards for dimensions, fenestration, and equipment. And the school might or might not boast such auxiliary facilities as auditoriums, lunchrooms, and gymnasiums. The only real variables were in the arrangement of the boxlike classrooms — should they be stacked up in a highrise building or strung out in a lowrise structure, should the building be compact or sprawling, corridored or corridorless? — and, of course, in architectural quality.

In the United States this collection-of-boxes, or egg-crate, approach to school design is more than a century old, dating back to 1847 and the construction of the Quincy School in Boston. Quincy is regarded as the first fully graded school to be built in the nation, that is, the first school in which pupils were divided by age and assigned in equal-sized groups to separate classrooms. Behind this departure from the multi-age groupings of the one-room schoolhouse was an educational philosophy premised on the self-contained classroom, in which one teacher guided the learning of groups ranging in size from 20 to as many as 60 pupils, the teacher-student ratio depending on the ability and willingness of the community to pay for education.

See Projects 3, 32, 43, 51, 52, 55, 56, 57, 58

Now, however, the egg-crate school is vanishing along with the educational philosophy that spawned it. The pattern has not totally disappeared, as some of the projects in this book will testify, and may never do so. School architecture will never again reflect the uncomplicated designing processes of the past. Behind the transformation of the schoolhouse is the realization that education is, or ought to be, a dynamic, continuously changing process. Perhaps belatedly, educators and architects alike realized that school design should accommodate this dynamism.

The process of change began in the early 1950s when educators — often with the stimulus and buying power provided by foundation funds — began experimenting with new educational arrangements such as team teaching, new techniques such as non-graded instruction, and new technology such as the use of educational television. It soon became evident that the traditional egg-crate schoolhouse stood in the way of experimentation. The standard, inflexible collection of boxlike classrooms did not lend itself to the new variably sized instructional groupings. Nor did it adapt well to the new instructional technology.

The Ford Foundation, which had backed much of the early educational experimentation, in 1958 decided to tackle the schoolhouse itself. For that purpose, the Foundation established and funded Educational Facilities Laboratories (EFL), whose mission is to "help American schools and colleges with their physical problems." EFL, where the author spent eight years as a staff member, pursues its mission in a variety of ways. Modest grants to school districts and colleges underwrite new approaches to facilities planning, a series of EFL-administered projects support research and experimentation in educational facilities design, and an active information program — including publications, films, exhibits, and other public relations efforts — disseminates the resulting knowledge.

It is difficult to assess the extent to which EFL's programs were responsible for the subsequent transformation in school planning and architecture. Had there been no EFL, necessity eventually might have generated change, but EFL's efforts very likely accelerated the process and provided an organization and direction to reform in school architecture that otherwise might have been lacking.

The important point is that, regardless of its causes, the transformation actually has occurred and, in effect, is documented in this book. No attempt was made to solicit examples of the new rather than the traditional schoolhouse for publication here. Instead, general invitations went to some 200 architectural firms participating in recent architectural exhibits of the American Association of School Administrators. Nevertheless, all but a handful of the nearly 200 designs — submitted by some 70 firms — represented departures, in varying degrees, from the traditional, stereotyped schoolhouse designs of the past.

The selection process for this book was not in the nature of an architectural competition; the author made no attempt to sit as a one-man jury. The final choice represents projects in which both school plan and available drawings serve to clearly illustrate specific stages in the evolution of schoolhouse design.

The reform in schoolhouse architecture was a direct outgrowth of reform in the educational process. Architectural responses were generated by varied and often drastic educational changes:

○ The curriculum was upgraded. Foreign languages and science were introduced in the elementary school. College-level courses were offered to capable high-school students. New approaches and techniques in reading, the schools' most critical problem, were adopted, and formal reading instruction was started earlier. Throughout the system, from kindergarten to college, educators concluded that students were capable of learning more and learning it earlier.

○ Utilization of teachers underwent reform as school system after school system began to experiment with such innovations as team teaching. Rather than spending all day with the same group of pupils, teachers were being employed in ways that best utilized their individual talents. And the teachers got help with the more routine and time-consuming aspects of their tasks when the schools began to utilize teacher trainees, aides, and clerks.

○ Teaching patterns were reformed, that is, the assumption that all children should proceed through the same subject material at the same pace — in a sort of educational lockstep — was junked. In its place, educators began to experiment with non-graded or continuous progress programs, in which individual students were encouraged to proceed at their own best pace.

○ Instructional groupings took new forms. Team teaching, non-graded and continuous-progress learning patterns did not fit into the fixed pupil capacity of the self-contained classroom. Instead, the new programs required large groups for lecture purposes, seminar groups for give and take, and "groups of one" for students who were handed greater responsibility for their own learning than in the traditional programs and the opportunity to pursue independent studies.

○ School scheduling also was affected. The 40- or 50-minute class period was no better suited to the new programs than was the self-contained classroom. In its place, educators turned to modular scheduling, in which the day was divided into shorter, 10- or 20-minute segments or modules. Individual programs were planned for each student, and each employed as many time modules as he required to complete an assignment or project.

○ School organization underwent change. Pressure for better racial integration in the schools and dissatisfaction with the educational effectiveness of the three-year high school called the structure of the junior high school into question. There was a movement to junk the old K-6, 7-9, 10-12 grade organization of the schools and replace it by middle or intermediate schools, which took a variety of grade organizational forms: 5-8, 6-8, 7-8, and so forth.

○ A new educational technology was introduced and educators began serious experimentation with its use in the schools. They often adopted such new developments as educational television, the electronic language laboratory or learning laboratory, study carrels equipped with dial-access systems for the retrieval of audio-taped or videotaped materials, programed teaching machines, and multimedia, rear-projection systems for large lecture groups. It appears that, ultimately, the computer itself will play an important role in the instructional process.

○ Racial integration played a role in the process of change, particularly in urban schools. Obvious solutions such as redrawing attendance zones, school pairing, and busing were not always effective. This led to experiments with the middle school, where integration could occur earlier in the pupil's life, with the educational park, where pupils were drawn from a large geographical area, and with the "magnet" school, in which educational excellence and specialized programs were intended to attract students from all areas of a city.

○ Finally, economics was a major factor in implementing all these programs. School systems everywhere faced difficulties just in providing enough new school space to meet enrollment growth and replace outmoded facilities. Given the chronic shortages of public funds, if the school systems were to provide facilities designed to house the new education they had to find economical ways of doing so.

The architectural response was as diverse as the educational pressures behind it. The essential problem, of course, was that in the egg-crate schoolhouse the walls literally stood in the way of educational reform because partitions between classroom boxes generally were either load-bearing or fabricated of masonry and plaster. In either case, it was difficult and often prohibitively expensive to alter the shape and size of teaching spaces to meet new requirements.

○ *New schools for the new education* might best describe the early architectural responses that were developed during the mid-1950s. Attempts were made to plan schools to meet the requirements of specific new educational programs. As an example, a school designed around team teaching might include large-group lecture halls, seminar rooms, a sprinkling of traditional classrooms, and spaces — in or out of the library — for independent study. These early departures from tradition had one great shortcoming: they were often as rigid and inflexible as their egg-crate predecessors. Any changes in administration or dissatisfaction with the current educational programs brought further reforms that called for new — or old — educational patterns to which, again, the schoolhouse was not adaptable. See Project 29

○ Operable partitions of the folding, sliding, or accordion types were seized upon as one answer. An early application was simply to install the partitions between pairs of classrooms, making it possible to convert instantly from traditional to large-group instructional patterns. In practice, these partitions seldom were employed as intended, and very often simply were left open all the time. See Projects 9, 24, 33, 35, 44, 55

See Projects
10, 11, 12,
15, 25, 26

○ New shapes for the schoolhouse began to appear as architects sought better applications of operable partitions, and struggled with the design of spaces suited to the use of new audio-visual techniques. Often the architects clustered spaces equivalent to three or four classrooms and, by employing operable partitions within the clusters, provided for a variety of instructional groupings. The results often were uneven because operable partitions frequently create problems in acoustical effectiveness and ease of operation, despite continuing technological improvements. They usually require built-in structural support and cannot be relocated easily, thus imposing their own restrictions on functional and architectural adaptability.

See Projects
1, 14, 17,
23, 30, 42,
48, 61

○ The loft plan provided a better solution for long-term or semipermanent applications. While operable partitions provided what might be called instant adaptability, the loft plan created a permanent flexibility. Within long, clear spans with a minimum of internal supporting columns, demountable partitions were installed to create spaces suited to whatever educational program was then in effect. When educational changes occurred, the walls could be relocated with relative ease and economy to accommodate the new programs.

○ The compact school was a logical outgrowth of the loft plan and of a concurrent trend toward air conditioning in schools; planners found that long spans were more practical and that air conditioning was less expensive to install and operate in compact buildings than in the sprawling ones then in vogue. Compactness was economical, particularly through reduction in perimeter wall area. At the same time, an air-conditioned compact building often had drastically reduced or even totally eliminated window area. The economies, however, were not enough to offset the fact that with conventional construction methods air-conditioned and loft-plan schools still were more expensive than the more traditional building forms.

See Projects
1, 17, 30

○ The systems approach was a response to that economic problem, as well as to political and generally ill-founded pressures to adopt stock plans for school construction in order to avoid or reduce architectural fees. The approach involved the development of modular, pre-engineered components that provided an economical, speedy method of erecting new schools, and ensured better quality construction. The systems, most developed under a series of EFL-sponsored projects, included structure, heating, ventilating, and cooling systems, ceiling and lighting, demountable and operable partitions, and cabinet-work. Strict performance specifications included the requirement that the components be totally compatible, permitting the architect to plug them together in an almost infinite variety of arrangements to suit his design requirements. Theoretically, the only restraint on the architect was that he work within the horizontal and vertical modules imposed by the system.

In effect, the component systems offered loft-plan flexibility, air conditioning, and high-quality materials at costs equal to or below those for conventional construction. The economies were achieved through in-factory mass production of the components and through reduction in on-site labor. Another systems approach advantage, speed of erection, made it possible to "deliver" a completed schoolhouse in significantly less time than possible under conventional construction methods.

○ Schools-without-walls are the most dramatic evidence of the trend toward adapting the schoolhouse to educational change. In many new schools, including a number published in this book, the classroom has given way to large, totally open zones of space accommodating as many as 200 or more pupils and their teachers. There are no partitions; movable furniture and/or screens provide visual privacy where desired. Acoustically absorbent ceilings and floors — that is, carpeted floors — ambient noise, and distance between groups provide acoustical privacy. These open spaces lend themselves to a wide variety of instructional groupings — from independent study to groups of 100 or more for lectures — and to instant and unobtrusive re-arrangement of the groupings. Schools-without-walls are adaptable to virtually any educational approach, traditional, team teaching, non-graded instruction, or the currently popular "open classroom" methods of the British infant schools.

See Projects
1, 14, 23,
42, 47, 50,
61

Beyond these basic developments, the plans described in this book offer evidence of other trends in schoolhouse planning. For example, the library, once nonexistent in the average elementary school or limited to a single, converted — and usually padlocked — classroom, has now become a major facility in most schools. Today, it houses not only books but a wide range of other media, and has been transformed from a citadel for books to an open area that invites use.

The school's auxiliary facilities are also changing. An outstanding example is the auditorium, once a single-purpose facility, a costly white elephant that stood empty most of the time. Operable partitions have changed all that. Today's school auditorium is likely to be in use for most of the day, and to be divisible into three or more acoustically private lecture halls of varying capacity, each fully equipped with modern audio-visual hardware. In finishings and furnishings, the emphasis has shifted away from security and inde-

See Projects
31, 39, 41, 53,
56

structibility toward comfort and amenity. Air conditioning is a commonplace and carpeting is coming into its own. Warm colors and textures have displaced the cold institutional ambience of the past. In short, the schoolhouse is becoming a place that welcomes children rather than incarcerates them.

See Projects
4, 5, 21,
35, 39, 52

And it is becoming a place that serves not only its pupils but the entire community. Once a single-purpose institution for students and their teachers, securely fenced and padlocked when classes were not in session, the schoolhouse increasingly is being designed for accessibility to the community. The ultimate — dispersal of the school through the community — may be suggested by the plan for the Human Resources Center in Pontiac, Michigan, published in this volume.

Project 21

See Project
55

Finally, there are new approaches to funding school construction. One is the use of air rights over highways, railroad yards, even the waterfront to avoid having to condemn valuable urban real estate and relocate residents — a costly and difficult social process. Another is joint occupancy, in which the air rights over new schools are sold or leased to the developers of commercial or residential buildings and the proceeds employed to defray the cost of building the schools.

The extent to which any new school design will reflect these trends is in only a minor way an architectural question. As this book suggests, some school systems still build egg-crate schools. Others have taken tentative, hesitant steps toward new schoolhouses for new education. And still others, like that in Pontiac, Michigan, have gone so far that they no longer think in terms of the schoolhouse as we have known it. The architect may help to educate his client to the available options, but the ultimate decision rests with the community, its school board, and its educators. It is they who develop the program that establishes the parameters within which the architect must work. In such a context, this book is an attempt to give architects and interested educators a representative selection of good, contemporary designs. The projects reproduced here reflect the diversity and dynamism characteristic both of today's education and today's schoolhouse architecture.

James J. Morisseau
September 1971

1 Birch School Addition

Owner Union Free School District No. 25, Merrick, New York

Administrator Dr. Robert C. Miles

Architects Caudill Rowlett Scott, Houston/New York/Hartford

Partner-in-charge Charles B. Thomsen

Project manager Peter Piven

Project designer William F. Schacht

Mechanical engineer Flack & Kurtz

Occupancy November 1970

Capacity 216

Organization K-2

Project costs $416,618 (including renovation of existing building)

Design and construction of this elementary school addition took only a year, largely because of a systems approach in which four key building subsystems — structure, roofing, ceiling-lighting, and heating-ventilating-air conditioning — were prebid on the basis of performance-type specifications. The addition essentially is a single, totally open space that made it possible for the school system to introduce team-teaching methods. Free-standing cabinetwork is employed to define areas within the overall space and to keep pupil groups to manageable proportions.

Floor plan:

1 Multi-instructional area
2 Staff
3 Conference
4 Existing school

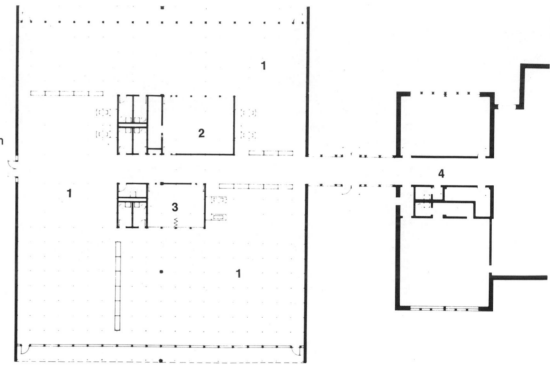

Section

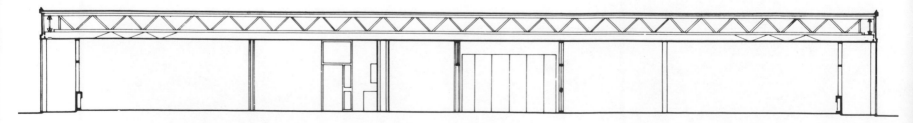

Multi-instructional area:

1 Custom cabinets (student storage, academic
   storage, teacher storage)
2 Study carrels
3 Modular tables
4 Conference table
5 Fixed cabinetry
6 Butcherblock tables
7 Informal seats
8 Easels
9 Platforms
10 Screens
11 Refrigerator

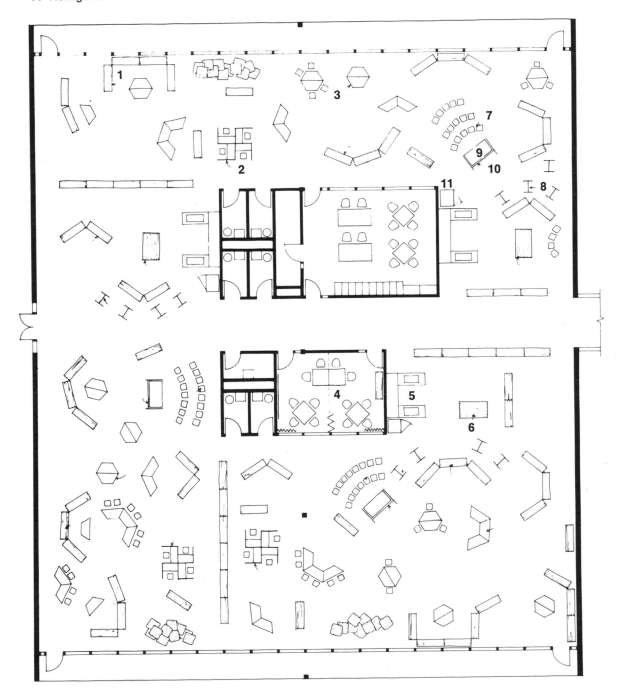

2 Jackson-Via Elementary School

Owner Charlottesville Public Schools, Charlottesville, Virginia

Superintendent Dr. Edward Rushton

Associated architects Caudill Rowlett Scott, Houston/New York/Hartford; Stainback & Scribner, Charlottesville, Virginia

Occupancy 1969

Capacity 712

Organization K-4

Construction costs $1,292,000

The house-plan approach here is applied to the elementary school. Operable partitions are employed in each four-classroom house to permit shifts from conventional classes to large-group instruction. Classrooms are carpeted; corridor and service areas are surfaced with quarry tile. Imaginative use of irregular site includes covered play area on lower level, convertible in the future to additional instructional space.

Lower level floor plan:

1 Covered play (future classroom cluster)
2 Theater
3 Activities
4 Mechanical
5 Boiler room

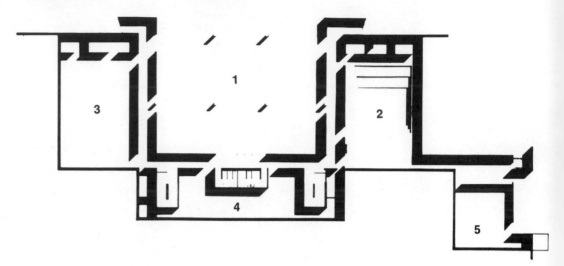

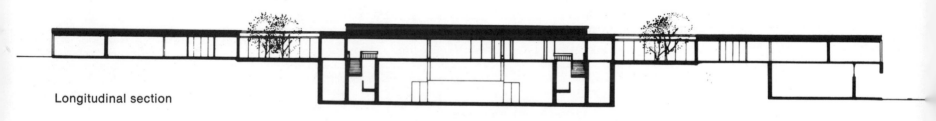

Longitudinal section

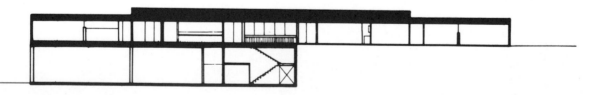

Cross section

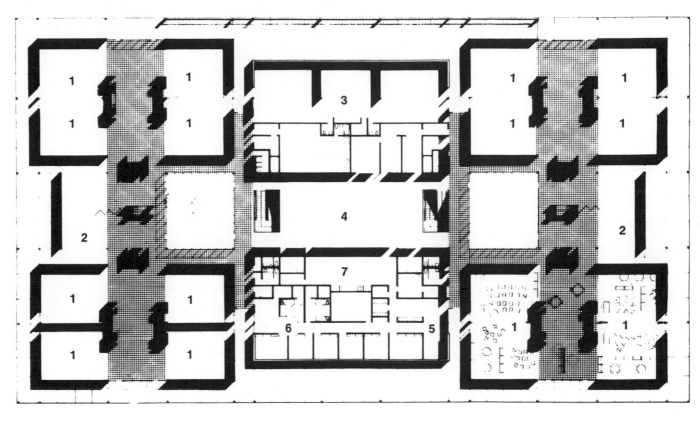

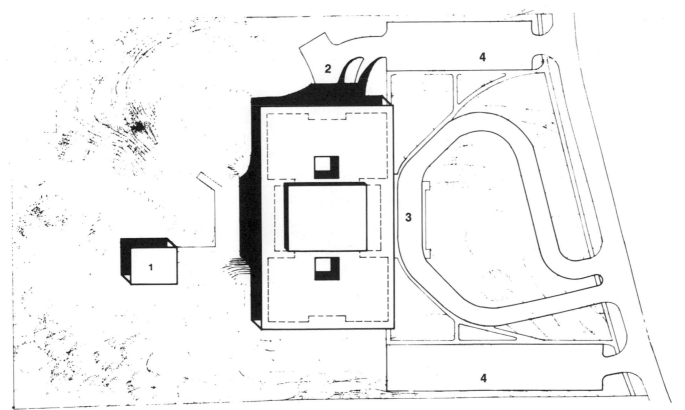

Ground floor plan:

1 Classroom
2 Kindergarten
3 Special education
4 Library
5 Administration
6 Health
7 Teachers' lounge

Site plan:

1 Play shed
2 Service
3 Entry
4 Parking

3 Primary School 380, Brooklyn

Owner New York City Board of Education, New York, New York

Chancellor Dr. Harvey B. Scribner

Architects Richard Dattner & Associates, New York, New York

Project architect Richard L. Carpenter

Mechanical engineer Arthur L. Zigas

Structural engineers Goldreich, Page & Thropp

Site engineers A. E. Bye & Associates

Occupancy 1972

Capacity 1,528

Organization K-4

Construction costs $7,000,000

This plan represents one of the first attempts in New York City to provide flexible spaces for variably sized instructional groupings. Large teaching complexes may be left open or may be divided, by demountable or operable partitions, into four regular classrooms. The building is designed to serve as part of the learning process: interior structure, ducts, conduits, and other mechanical features are exposed, and the color-coded boiler room will be open for student visits.

First floor plan:

1 Kindergarten classrooms
2 Large group room
3 Administration
4 Health
5 Auditorium
6 Gymnasium
7 Cafeteria
8 Teachers' lunchroom
9 Kitchen
10 Community room

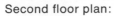

Second floor plan:

1 Teaching complex
2 Art classroom
3 Art and science workroom
4 Speech
5 Library
6 Administration
7 Junior guidance
8 Special education

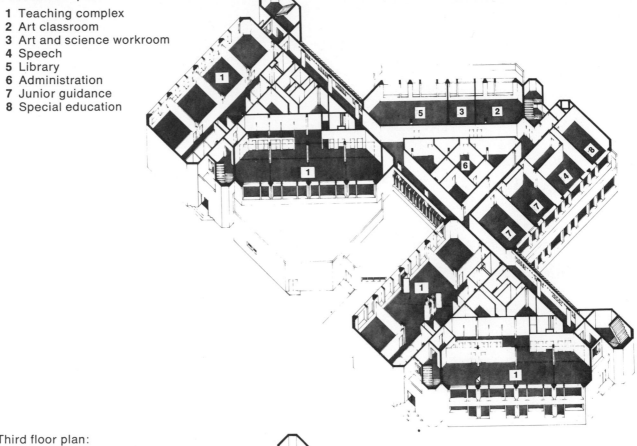

Third floor plan:

1 Teaching complex
2 Junior guidance
3 Special education

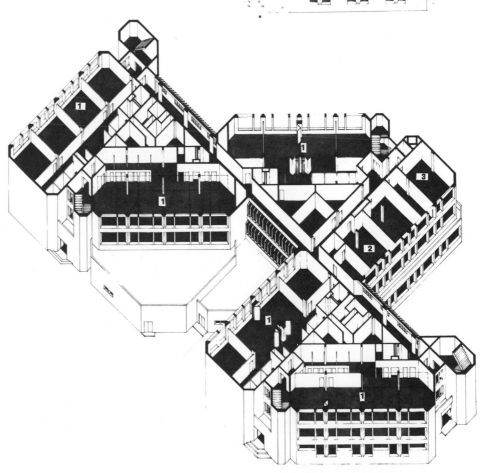

4 Minot-Hemenway School

Owner Boston Public Schools, Boston, Massachusetts

Superintendent William H. Ohrenberger

Architects Samuel, Glaser and Partners, Boston, Massachusetts

Partner-in-charge Antonio P. deCastro

Project designer Mary Ellen Quirk

Job captain Vilnis Bebrekarklis

Structural engineers Cleverdon, Varney & Pike

Mechanical-electrical engineers Borek Associates, Inc.

Landscape Shurcliff, Merrill & Footit

Occupancy 1973

Capacity 1,000

Organization K-5

Project costs $6,000,000

This urban elementary school, planned for community use, is divided into three academic houses and a multi-use community center. An early childhood house (usually kindergarten and first grade) is subdivided into two team centers of 150 pupils each and, within the centers, into clusters of two classes each. Both the primary house (grades two and three) and the elementary house (grades four and five) are subdivided into two team centers and, within the centers, to clusters of three class groups focused around a project area. The community center, including library, swimming pool, cafetorium, and music facilities, can be closed off from the academic wing after school hours.

First floor plan:
1 Kindergarten
2 First grade
3 Administration
4 Cafetorium
5 Kitchen
6 Music rooms
7 Swimming pool

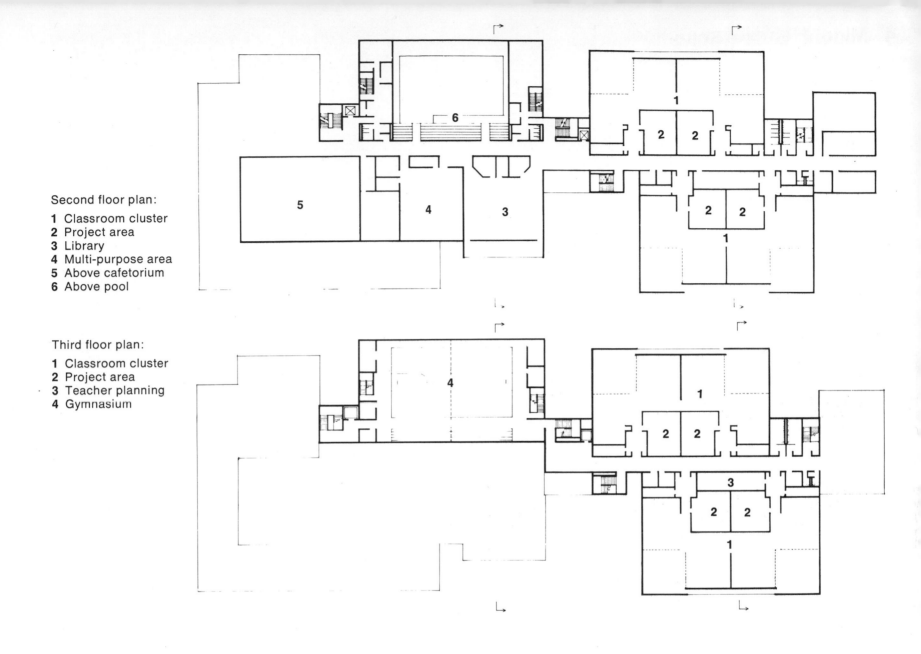

Second floor plan:

1 Classroom cluster
2 Project area
3 Library
4 Multi-purpose area
5 Above cafetorium
6 Above pool

Third floor plan:

1 Classroom cluster
2 Project area
3 Teacher planning
4 Gymnasium

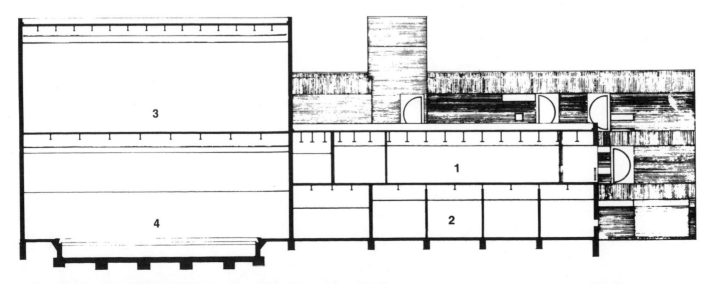

Cross section:

1 Library
2 Administration
3 Gymnasium
4 Swimming pool

17

5 Joseph E. Lee School

Owner Boston Public Schools, Boston, Massachusetts

Superintendent William H. Ohrenberger

Architects Isidor Richmond and Carney Goldberg, Boston

Structural engineers Patti Associates

Mechanical-electrical engineers Francis Associates, Inc.

Occupancy September 1971

Capacity 1,100

Organization K-5

Project costs $7,800,000

Construction costs $5,610,594

Clusters of six open classrooms grouped around a common learning area dominate the plan for this new, specialized urban elementary school. To create and enhance pupil identity, a hierarchy of groups — from 25 in a class, to 75 in a cluster, to 150 in a house — is provided for. Like other new Boston elementary schools this one will be specialized, concentrating on the theater arts, speech, and music. The school also is designed as a community facility with public spaces in operation 14 hours a day.

First floor plan:
 1 Kindergartens
 2 Classrooms
 3 Advanced class
 4 Special class
 5 Teachers' room
 6 Arts and projects
 7 Exhibition space
 8 Administration
 9 Guidance
10 Health
11 Multi-purpose room
12 Stage
13 Music room
14 Gymnasium
15 Swimming pool
16 Faculty dining
17 Kitchen
18 Lobby
19 Loading
20 Parking

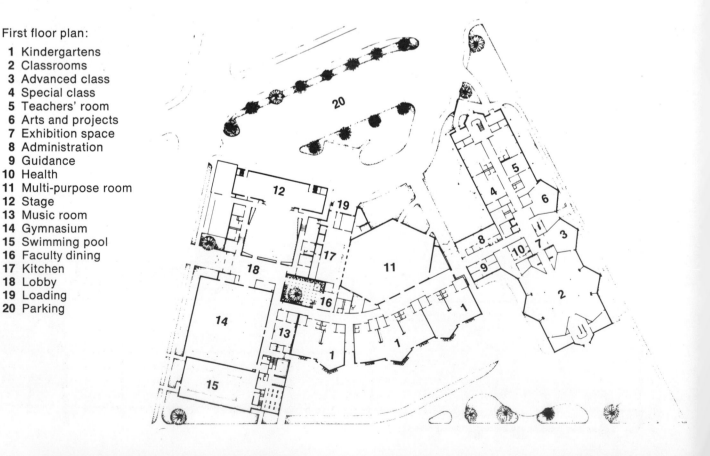

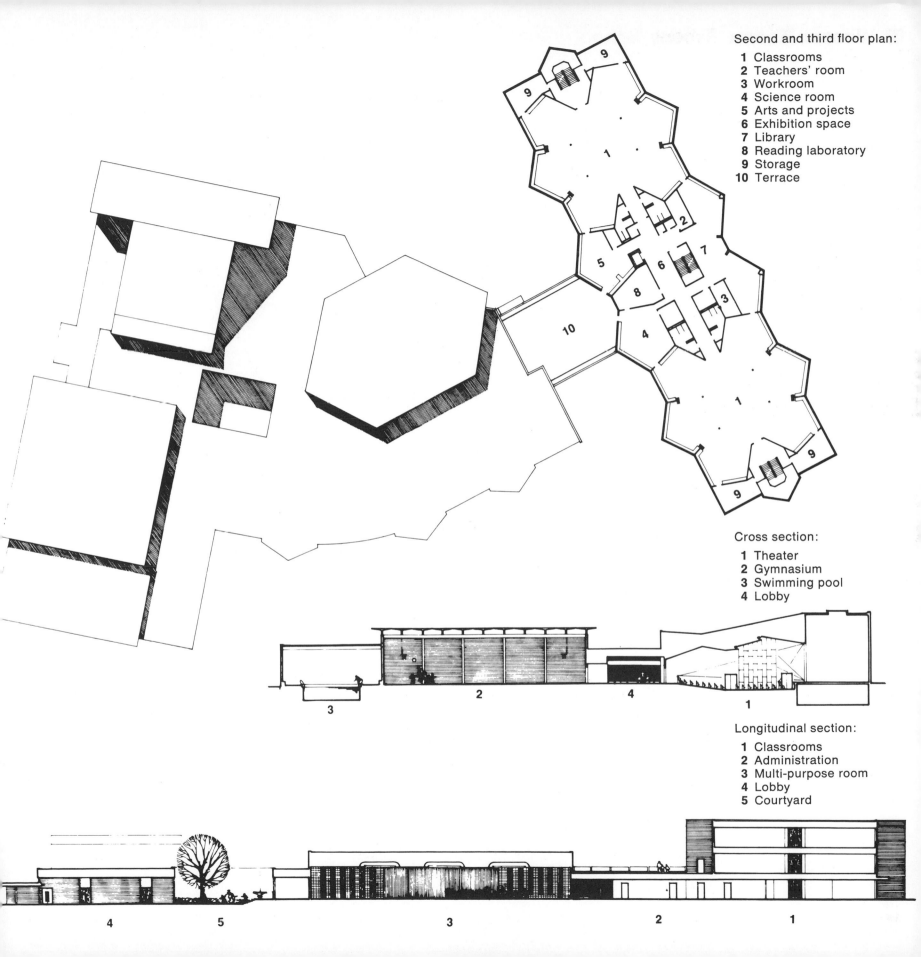

Second and third floor plan:

1 Classrooms
2 Teachers' room
3 Workroom
4 Science room
5 Arts and projects
6 Exhibition space
7 Library
8 Reading laboratory
9 Storage
10 Terrace

Cross section:

1 Theater
2 Gymnasium
3 Swimming pool
4 Lobby

Longitudinal section:

1 Classrooms
2 Administration
3 Multi-purpose room
4 Lobby
5 Courtyard

6 William Monroe Trotter School

Owner Boston Public Schools, Boston, Massachusetts

Superintendent William H. Ohrenberger

Principal Leo Howard

Architects Drummey Rosane Anderson, Inc., Newton Lower Falls, Massachusetts

Principal-in-charge David W. Anderson

Project designers Martin Pitt, Terrence McCormick

Structural engineers Nichols, Norton & Zaldastani, Inc.

Mechanical-electrical engineers Francis Associates

Occupancy September 1969

Capacity 750

Organization Preschool-6

Project costs $2,649,684

Construction costs $2,150,000

The form of this urban elementary school grew out of a highly imaginative educational program and resulted in the concept of four educational pods, each with six paired classrooms surrounding a learning laboratory. Ancillary facilities include a large playroom, a guidance suite, and an auditorium. A prekindergarten program and facilities are provided, along with space for a college instructional team, who will observe the school's programs and instruct inner-city teachers.

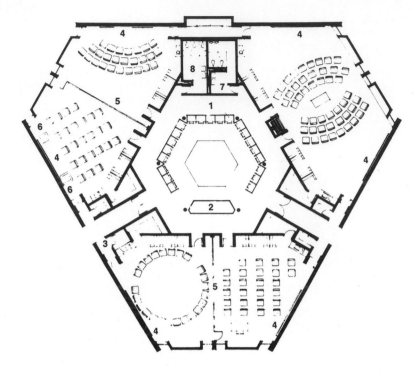

Classroom pod:
1 Study carrels
2 Learning wall
3 Observation
4 Chalkboard
5 Operable wall with chalkboard
6 TV
7 Boys
8 Girls

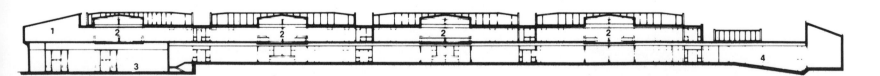

Longitudinal section:
1 Classroom
2 Learning laboratory
3 Playroom
4 Auditorium

Lower floor plan:

1 Playroom	**8** Offices	**15** Kitchen
2 Kindergartens	**9** Guidance	**16** Music
3 Prekindergarten	**10** Conference	**17** Lobby
4 Remedial reading	**11** Work area	**18** Mechanical
5 Speech	**12** Auditorium	**19** Entrance court
6 Art	**13** Health	**20** Kindergarten playcourt
7 Library	**14** Cafeteria	**21** Garden

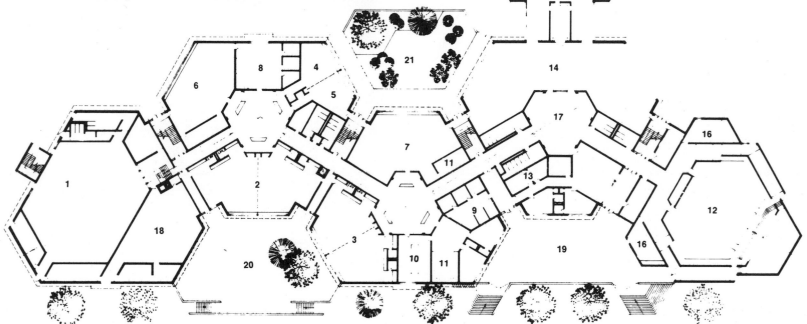

Upper floor plan:

1 Classroom
2 Learning laboratory
3 Preparation
4 Lounge

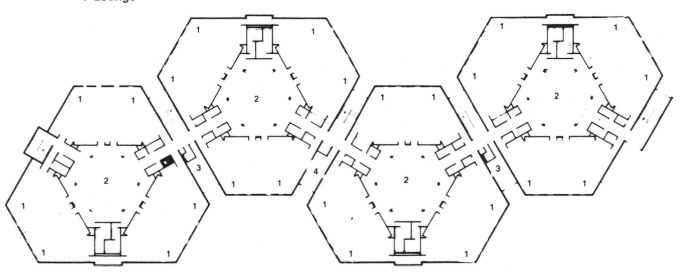

7 Orr Elementary School Replacement

Owner Board of Education, District of Columbia

Superintendent Dr. Hugh Scott

Architects Louis C. Kingscott & Associates, Inc., Kalamazoo, Michigan

Project architect Donald Roberts

Occupancy not scheduled

Capacity 750

Organization Preschool, K-6

Construction costs $1,893,000

Open learning centers accommodating 220 pupils each, a program and facilities for preschool children, and indoor and outdoor facilities for community use highlight this plan for an urban elementary school. The building is designed for expansion; provision has been made for the addition of a fifth floor to accommodate another learning center, increasing ultimate enrollment capacity to about 960.

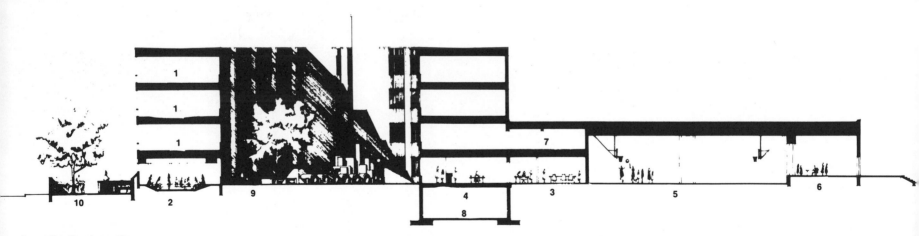

Longitudinal section:
1 Learning center
2 Kindergarten
3 Resources
4 Administration
5 All-purpose room
6 Stage
7 Storage-mechanical
8 Basement mechanical
9 Inner court
10 Outer court

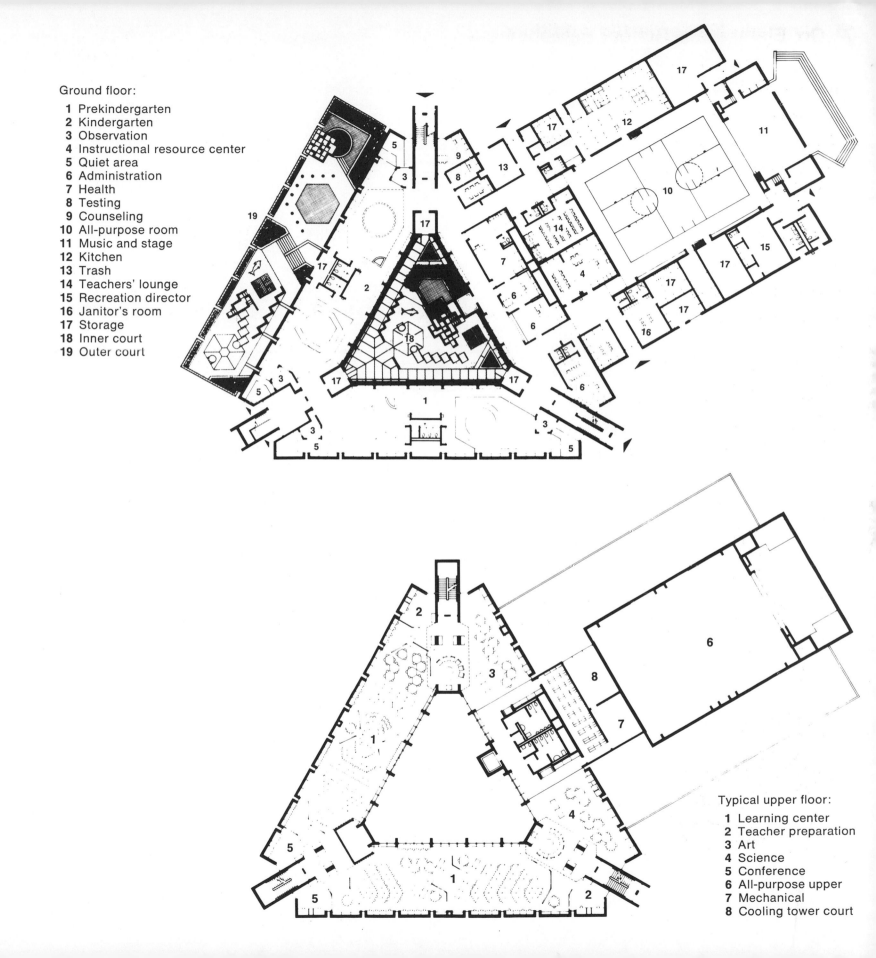

Ground floor:

 1 Prekindergarten
 2 Kindergarten
 3 Observation
 4 Instructional resource center
 5 Quiet area
 6 Administration
 7 Health
 8 Testing
 9 Counseling
10 All-purpose room
11 Music and stage
12 Kitchen
13 Trash
14 Teachers' lounge
15 Recreation director
16 Janitor's room
17 Storage
18 Inner court
19 Outer court

Typical upper floor:

1 Learning center
2 Teacher preparation
3 Art
4 Science
5 Conference
6 All-purpose upper
7 Mechanical
8 Cooling tower court

8 Nineteen Kindergarten Additions

Owner Chesterfield County School Board, Virginia

Superintendent Dr. Robert F. Kelly

Architects Hyland & Highfill, Richmond, Virginia

Mechanical-electrical engineers William G. Brandt & Associates

Structural engineer Alvin W. Dunbar

Occupancy 1968

Capacity variable

Organization K and K-6

Construction costs $2,000,000

A decision in the mid-1960s to add kindergarten programs to this county-wide system brought with it a requirement for additions to 19 existing elementary schools. After weighing the alternatives, the district opted to hire one architectural firm to design all 19. The result was a basic, octagonal design providing a range of sizes, arrangements, and pupil capacity. The additions can serve the kindergarten program, the upper grades, or a combination of both, or be adapted to serve such needs as library space.

Instructional materials center:

1 Library classroom
2 Conference
3 Office
4 Story telling
5 Audio-visual area
6 Books

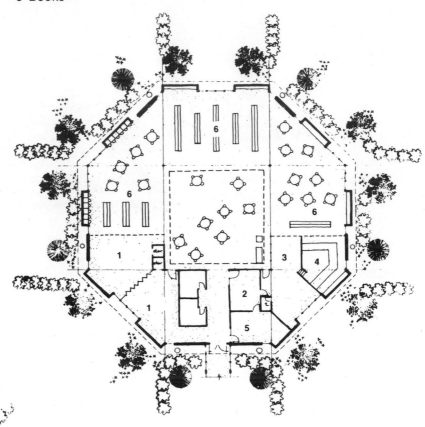

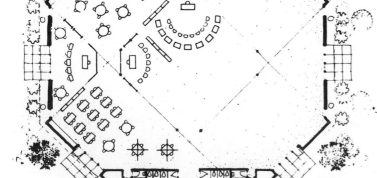

250-pupil instructional block:

1 Group instruction area
2 Boys
3 Girls

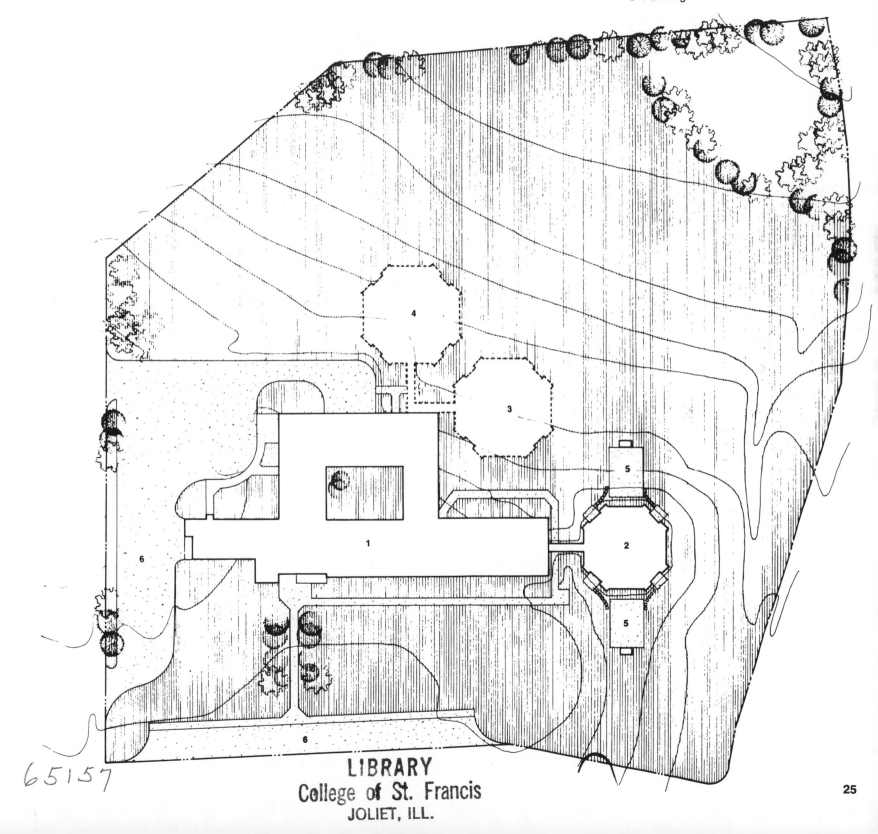

Site plan:
1 Existing building
2 Addition
3 Possible new instructional addition
4 Possible library addition
5 Play area
6 Parking

65157

LIBRARY
College of St. Francis
JOLIET, ILL.

9 Northside Elementary School/Hamilton Road Elementary School

Owner Board of Education, Fairport, New York

Superintendent Dr. W. McGregor Deller

Principal Gary Dunton

Architects Parks, Morin, Hall, Brennan & Sattelberg, Rochester, New York

Occupancy December 1970

Capacity 2,150

Organization K-6

Project costs $5,678,000

Construction costs $3,593,329

Two schools, one for the primary grades and the other for intermediate grades, share a site and common facilities in this plan. In layout, the schools represent a not-uncommon compromise between the self-contained classroom and open planning. Paired classrooms divided by operable partitions offer some flexibility in groupings. Independent and small group study is possible in the schools' libraries, and a lecture hall and the cafeteria accommodate large-group instruction. All interior partitioning is demountable to provide for long-term flexibility.

Site plan:

1 Primary
2 Intermediate
3 Shared facilities
4 Parking

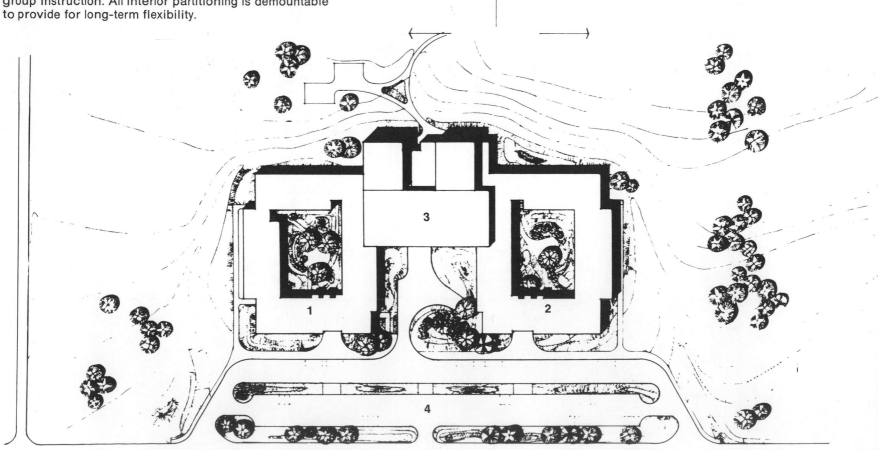

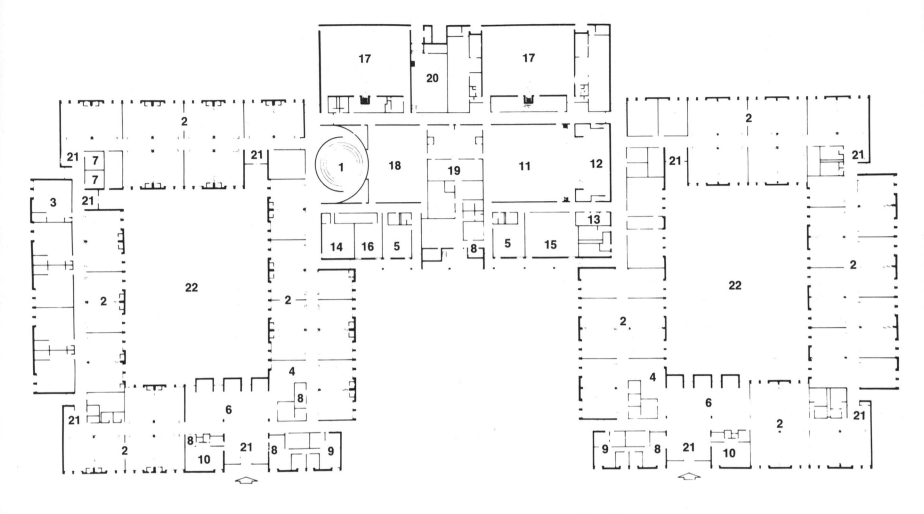

Floor plan:

1 Large-group instruction
2 Classroom wings
3 Kindergartens
4 Study area
5 Faculty
6 Library
7 Reading
8 Office
9 Conference
10 Health
11 Auditorium-gym station

12 Stage
13 Practice rooms
14 Primary music
15 Intermediate music
16 Art
17 Gymnasium
18 Cafeteria-gym station
19 Kitchen
20 Boiler
21 Lobby
22 Court

Owner The School District of Philadelphia, Philadelphia, Pennsylvania

Superintendent Dr. Mark R. Shedd

Architects Anthony T. Rienzi & Associates, Philadelphia, Pennsylvania

Structural engineers Schulcz & Padlasky

Mechanical engineers Robert G. Werden & Associates

Occupancy September 1972

Capacity 970

Organization K-6

Project costs $2,500,000

Construction costs $2,117,625

The basic teaching unit in this urban elementary school is a triangular classroom. The units are clustered in groups of five and separated by operable partitions to provide flexibility in instructional groupings. The design provides for controlled community use of such facilities as the gymnasium, auditorium, and community room — at any time during the day or evening — which does not disrupt school functions.

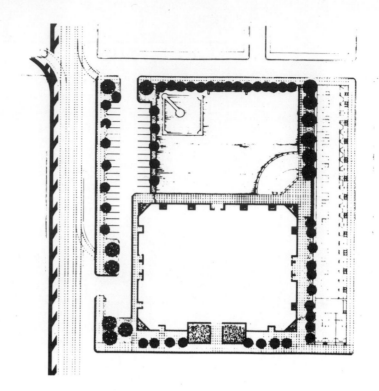

Site plan

Longitudinal section:
1 Library
2 Cafeteria
3 Auditorium
4 Gymnasium

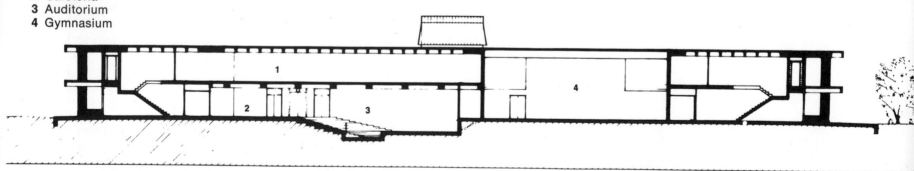

Cross section:
1 Locker room
2 Classroom cluster

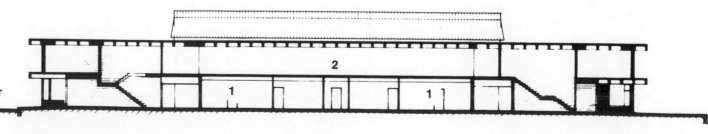

First floor plan:

1 Kindergarten
2 Prekindergarten
3 Science classroom
4 Creative arts
5 Administration
6 Health
7 Auditorium
8 Music classroom
9 Practice room
10 Gymnasium
11 Cafeteria
12 Faculty dining
13 Serving
14 Community room
15 Lobby
16 Mechanical room

Second floor plan:

1 Classroom cluster
2 Team-planning room
3 Special education classroom
4 Small class instruction
5 Teachers' lounge and workroom
6 Instructional materials center
7 Librarian's office and workroom
8 Individual progress instruction storage
9 Materials production area
10 TV room
11 Audio-visual work and storage
12 Open upper part of gymnasium

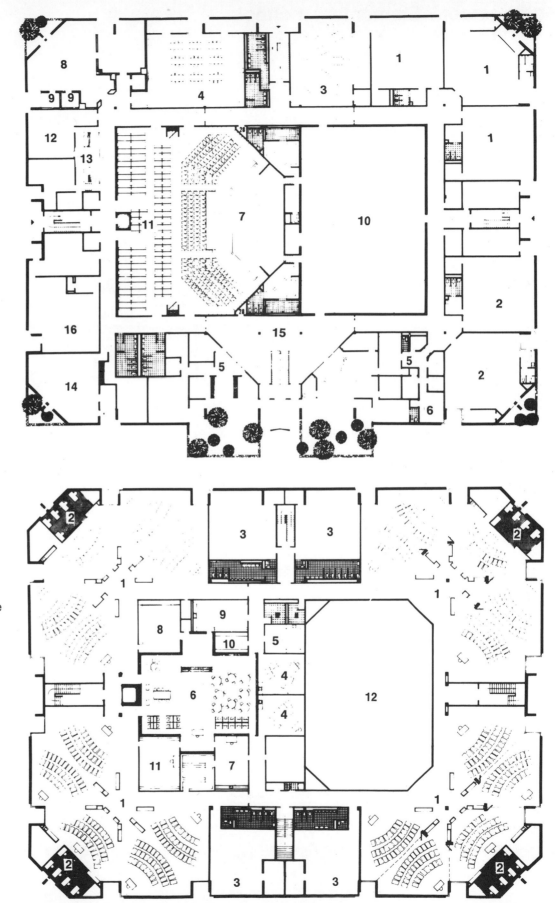

29

11 Southeastern Elementary School

Owner Eaton Rapids Public Schools, Eaton Rapids, Michigan

Superintendent W. Carl Holbrook

Principal Don Lockwood

Architects Louis C. Kingscott & Associates, Kalamazoo, Michigan

Project architect Brooks H. Godfrey

Occupancy September 1970

Capacity 600

Organization K-6

Project costs $943,005

Construction costs $748,451

The basic instructional module in this elementary-school plan is a three-classroom unit for 75 to 90 pupils. Designed to operate as open, team teaching spaces, the units are equipped with one operable partition for use when audio-visual programs or other noise-generating activities are scheduled. Of functional and economic interest is the instructional materials center which doubles in brass as a major part of the school's circulation space.

Floor plan:

1 Three-classroom unit
2 Kindergarten
3 Planning
4 Conference
5 Instructional materials center
6 Office
7 Multi-purpose room
8 Dressing rooms
9 Kitchen
10 Boiler room
11 Mechanical

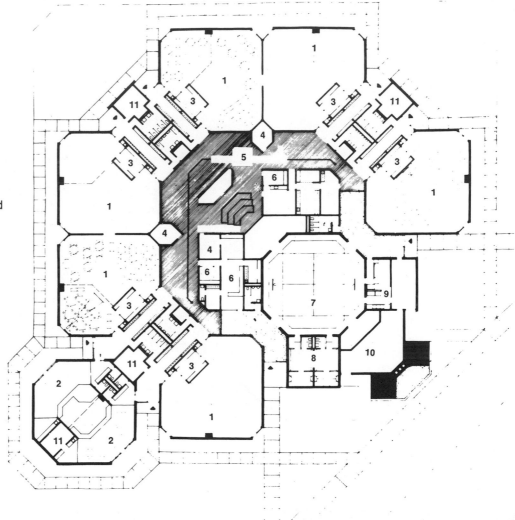

Section:

1 Instructional materials center
2 Instructional materials study area
3 Multi-purpose room
4 Audio-visual control
5 Storage
6 Boiler
7 Corridor

12 Rushwood Elementary School

Owner Nordonia Hills Local School District, Sagamore Hills, Ohio

Superintendent William J. Boliantz

Principal Harold A. Meese

Architects Ross-Yamane Associates, Cleveland, Ohio

Structural engineers R. M. Gensert Associates

Mechanical engineers Paul Colton & Associates

Electrical engineers Charles A. Lewis & Associates

Civil engineers Hedrick-Cox-Dancull

Occupancy September 1970

Capacity 860

Organization K-6

Project costs $1,069,453

Construction costs $924,918

Designed for a non-graded, team-teaching program, this school is planned around a series of open classroom pods accommodating 90 to 120 pupils each. An area within each pod can be closed off by an operable partition to provide visual and acoustical privacy for audio-visual presentations. The pods are designed to accommodate conversion to self-contained classrooms, should that become desirable. A large library, equipped with individual study carrels and group-study areas, is at the school's core.

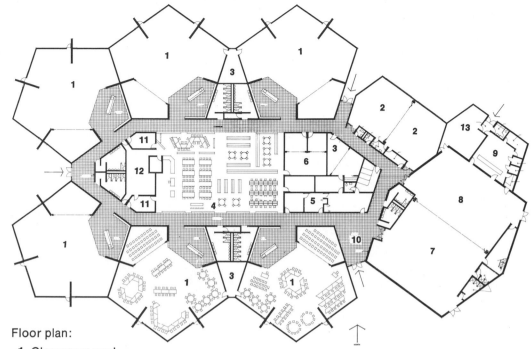

Floor plan:

1 Classroom pod
2 Kindergarten
3 Staff planning
4 Library and learning resources center
5 Administration
6 Conference
7 Multi-purpose room
8 Cafeteria and special purpose classroom
9 Kitchen
10 Corridor-lobby area
11 Planning and storage
12 Audio-visual storage and work area
13 Mechanical equipment

Longitudinal section:

1 Library and learning center
2 Administration
3 Multi-purpose room
4 Showers
5 Toilets
6 Audio-visual storage and work
7 Storage
8 Lobby

Cross section:

1 Classroom pod
2 Planning and storage

13 Ridge Hill School

Owner Town of Hamden, Connecticut

Superintendent Dr. Frank R. Yulo

Principal Val Bernardoni

Architects Harold Roth and Edward Saad, Hamden, Connecticut

Structural engineers Associated Engineering

Mechanical engineers Hubbard, Lawless & Osborne

Landscape Peter Rolland Associates

Lighting Sylvan R. Shemitz

Acoustics Bolt, Beranek & Newman

Occupancy January 1971

Capacity 1,166

Organization K-6

Project costs $4,900,000

Construction costs $3,300,000

Split-level "learning center units" for about 125 pupils each are the key elements in this plan for a non-graded, continuous-progress elementary school. The open units are carpeted and have either raised platforms, small, sunken amphitheaters, or both to provide for a variety of groupings. Each has its own conference room, maintenance and storage closets, lavatories, and wardrobes to provide maximum self-sufficiency.

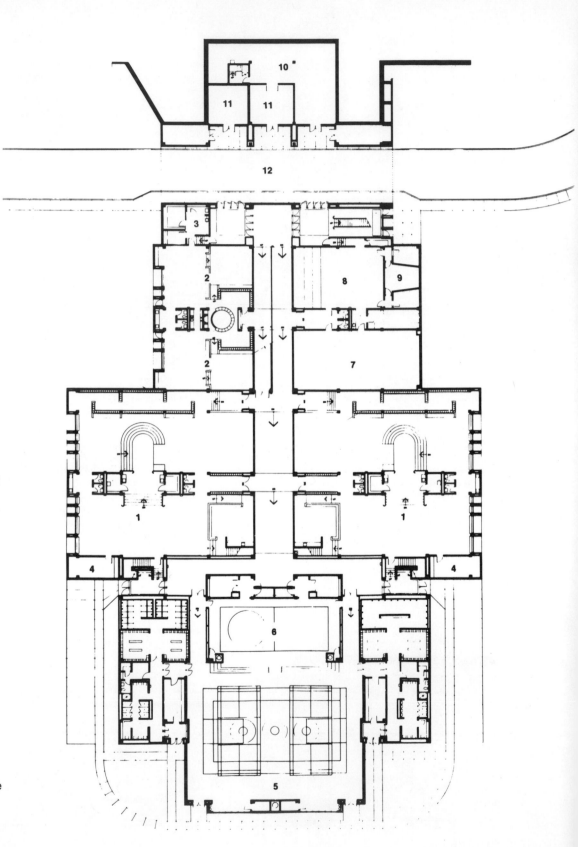

Lower level floor plan:

1 Learning center unit
2 Kindergarten
3 Workroom
4 Conference
5 Gymnasium-auditorium
6 Exercise room and stage
7 Audio-visual center
8 Music room
9 Practice room
10 Mechanical equipment
11 Electrical equipment
12 Bus drive

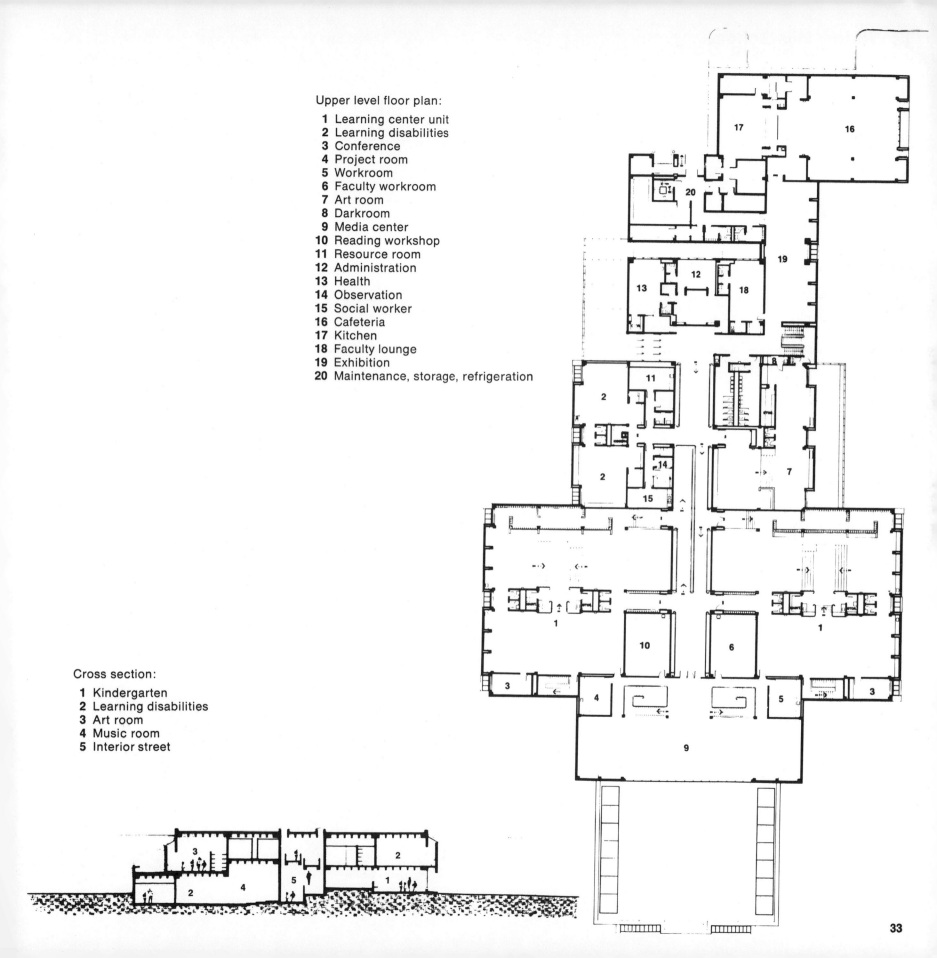

Upper level floor plan:

1 Learning center unit
2 Learning disabilities
3 Conference
4 Project room
5 Workroom
6 Faculty workroom
7 Art room
8 Darkroom
9 Media center
10 Reading workshop
11 Resource room
12 Administration
13 Health
14 Observation
15 Social worker
16 Cafeteria
17 Kitchen
18 Faculty lounge
19 Exhibition
20 Maintenance, storage, refrigeration

Cross section:

1 Kindergarten
2 Learning disabilities
3 Art room
4 Music room
5 Interior street

14 Laguna-Riviera School

Owner Carlsbad Unified School District, Carlsbad, California

Superintendent Dr. Howard C. Harmon

Architects Ruhnau, Evans & Steinmann, Riverside, California

Structural engineers Brandow & Johnston Associates

Electrical engineers Sampson, Randall & Press

Mechanical engineers Nack & Sunderland

Civil engineers Albert A. Webb & Associates

Landscape Roy H. Seifert & Associates

Occupancy not scheduled

Capacity 690

Organization K-6

Project costs $1,020,000

Construction costs $855,600

In this modern version of the one-room schoolhouse, virtually all instruction for nearly 700 pupils occurs in one vast, loftlike room. Only teacher preparation and special-instruction spaces are enclosed. Movable chalkboards and vision panels will be employed to provide visual privacy where required. As something of a hedge of the school district's bets, the physical plant is designed to permit conversion to a conventional classroom layout.

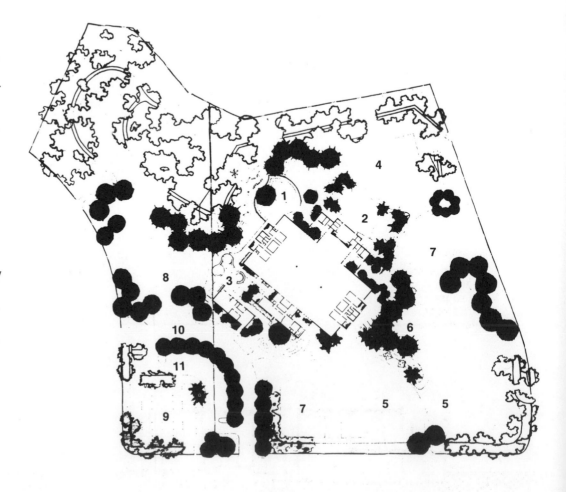

Site plan:
1 Kindergarten
2 Amphitheater
3 Lunch
4 Primary play
5 Upper grade play
6 Play
7 Paved play
8 Community park
9 Tennis courts
10 Bus pickup
11 Parking

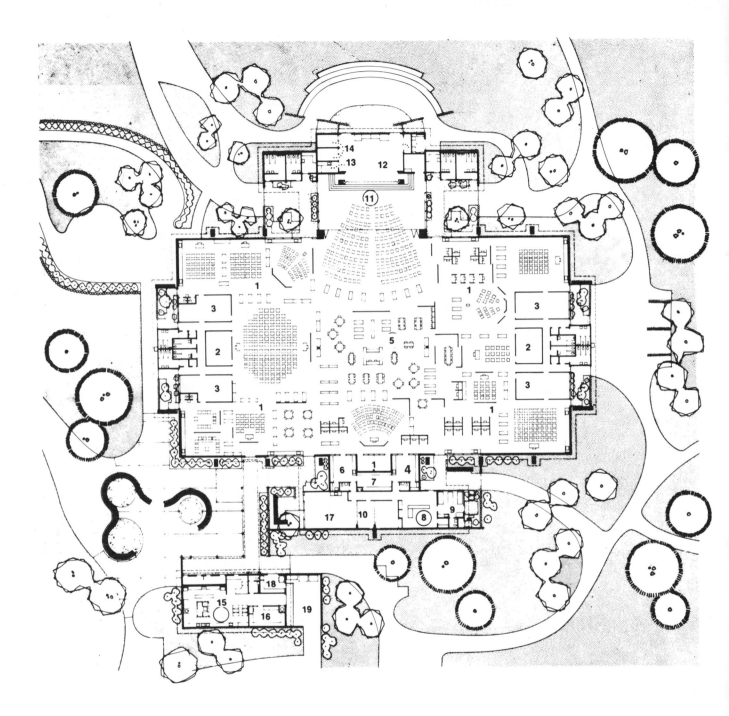

Floor plan:

1 Group instruction
2 Special instruction
3 Teacher preparation
4 Teachers' workroom
5 Resource center
6 Book repair
7 Book storage
8 Administration
9 Health
10 Conference

11 Multi-purpose area
12 Band platform
13 Control room
14 Practice
15 Kitchen
16 Food service
17 Teachers' lounge
18 Maintenance
19 Service yard

15 William C. Longstreth Public School

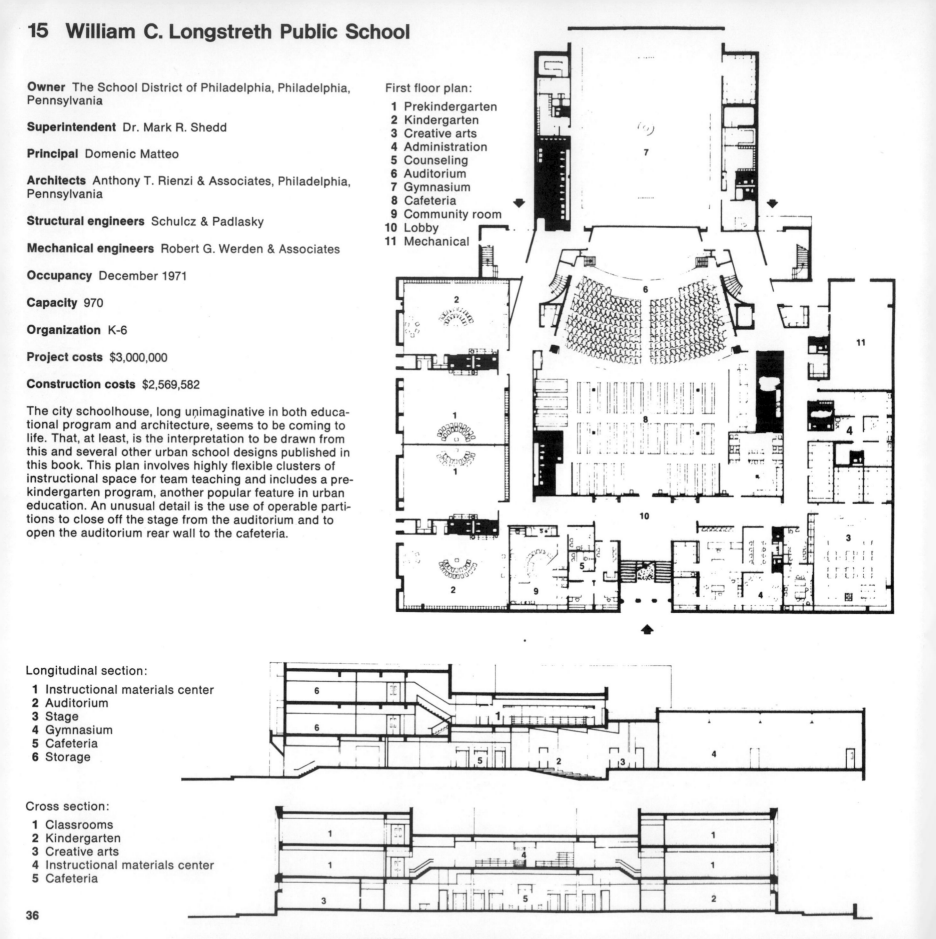

Owner The School District of Philadelphia, Philadelphia, Pennsylvania

Superintendent Dr. Mark R. Shedd

Principal Domenic Matteo

Architects Anthony T. Rienzi & Associates, Philadelphia, Pennsylvania

Structural engineers Schulcz & Padlasky

Mechanical engineers Robert G. Werden & Associates

Occupancy December 1971

Capacity 970

Organization K-6

Project costs $3,000,000

Construction costs $2,569,582

The city schoolhouse, long unimaginative in both educational program and architecture, seems to be coming to life. That, at least, is the interpretation to be drawn from this and several other urban school designs published in this book. This plan involves highly flexible clusters of instructional space for team teaching and includes a prekindergarten program, another popular feature in urban education. An unusual detail is the use of operable partitions to close off the stage from the auditorium and to open the auditorium rear wall to the cafeteria.

First floor plan:
1 Prekindergarten
2 Kindergarten
3 Creative arts
4 Administration
5 Counseling
6 Auditorium
7 Gymnasium
8 Cafeteria
9 Community room
10 Lobby
11 Mechanical

Longitudinal section:
1 Instructional materials center
2 Auditorium
3 Stage
4 Gymnasium
5 Cafeteria
6 Storage

Cross section:
1 Classrooms
2 Kindergarten
3 Creative arts
4 Instructional materials center
5 Cafeteria

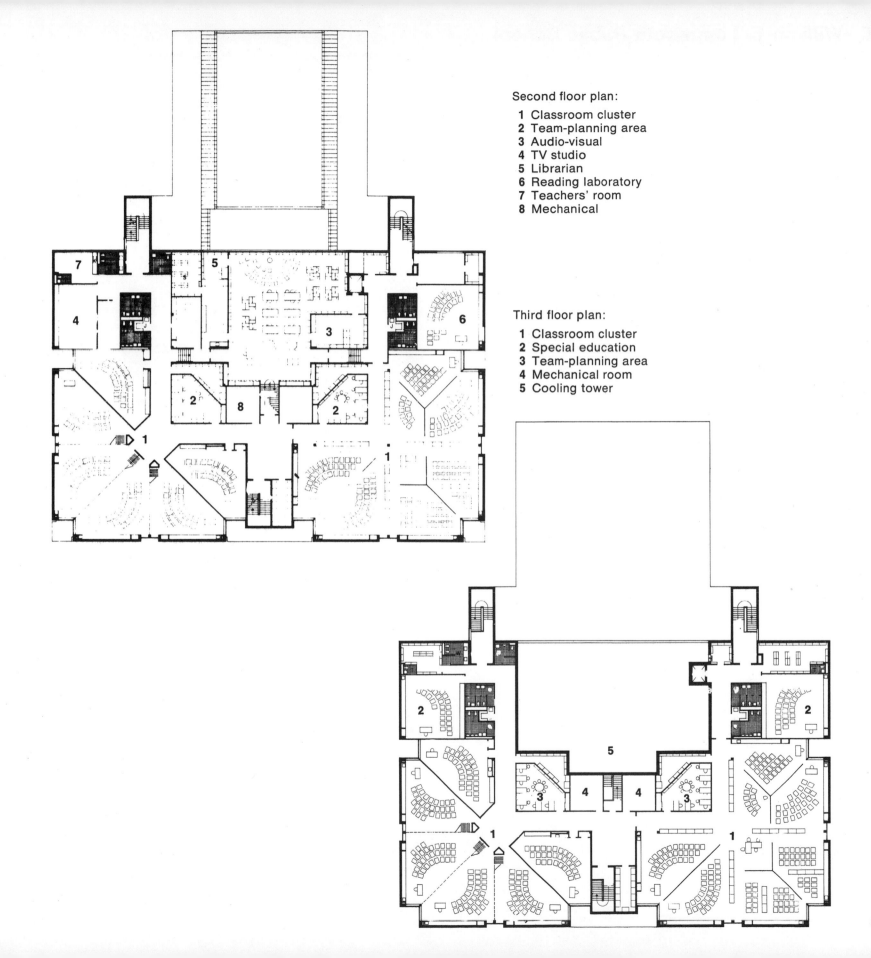

Second floor plan:

1 Classroom cluster
2 Team-planning area
3 Audio-visual
4 TV studio
5 Librarian
6 Reading laboratory
7 Teachers' room
8 Mechanical

Third floor plan:

1 Classroom cluster
2 Special education
3 Team-planning area
4 Mechanical room
5 Cooling tower

16 Merriam Elementary School

Owner Unified School District No. 512, Shawnee Mission, Kansas

Superintendent Dr. Arzell Hall

Principal Fred Hunter, Jr.

Architects Marshall & Brown of Kansas, Kansas City, Kansas

Project architect Jack E. Lakey

Structural engineer F. A. Towner

Mechanical-electrical engineers Holloway, Perkins & Eisman

Occupancy September 1969

Capacity 400

Organization K-6

Construction costs $682,000

Open spaces and operable partitions are combined in this design to provide variety in teaching arrangements. Each of three teaching suites can be divided into four autonomous classrooms, which can be further subdivided by rolling storage dividers or can be opened up into large lecture halls. Teachers' offices are equipped with a one-way observation window to facilitate supervision of the students.

Lower floor plan:
1 Lunchroom
2 Kitchen
3 Mechanical

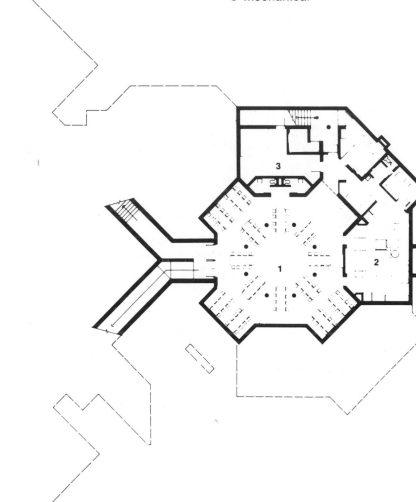

Cross section:
1 Kindergarten
2 Teachers' workroom
3 Kitchen

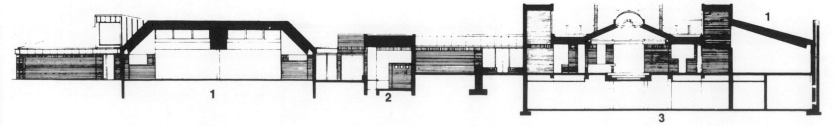

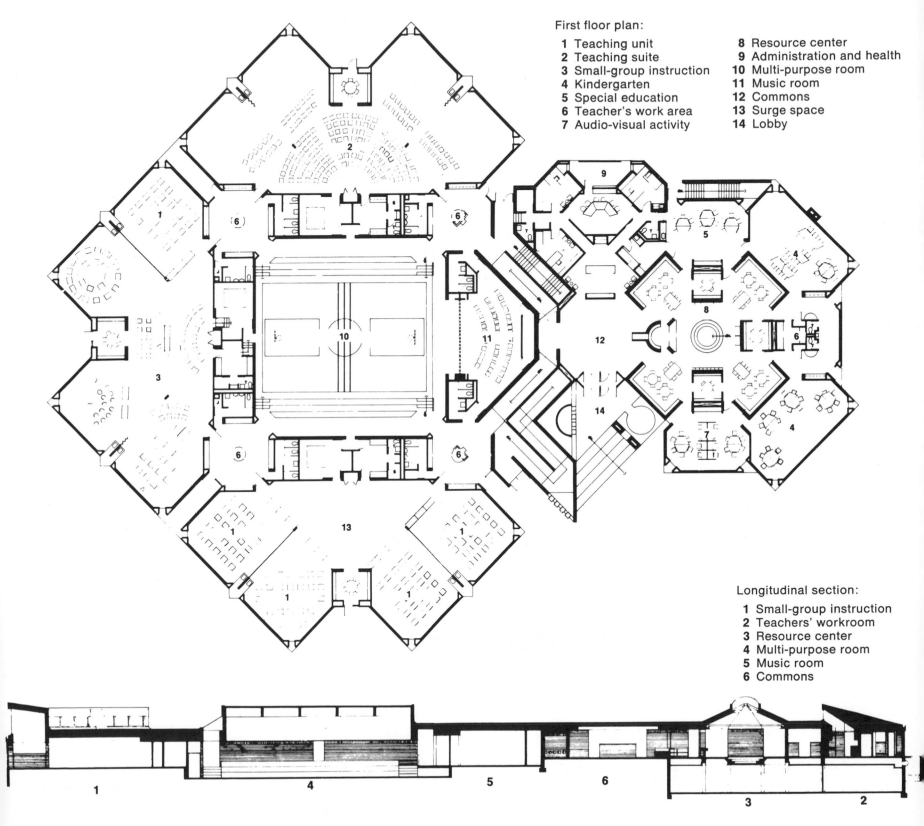

First floor plan:

1 Teaching unit
2 Teaching suite
3 Small-group instruction
4 Kindergarten
5 Special education
6 Teacher's work area
7 Audio-visual activity
8 Resource center
9 Administration and health
10 Multi-purpose room
11 Music room
12 Commons
13 Surge space
14 Lobby

Longitudinal section:

1 Small-group instruction
2 Teachers' workroom
3 Resource center
4 Multi-purpose room
5 Music room
6 Commons

17 DeLaveaga Elementary School

Owner Santa Cruz City Schools, Santa Cruz, California

Superintendent Denzil Morrisey

Principal Malcolm Macaulay

Architects Leefe & Ehrenkrantz, San Francisco, California

Structural engineer Charles M. Herd

Mechanical engineers G. L. Gendler & Associates

Electrical engineer Stanley Anderson

Educational consultants Odell MacConnell Associates

Occupancy October 1966

Capacity 600

Organization K-6

Construction costs $650,630

One of the original project schools erected under the
School Construction Systems Development project in
California, this elementary school is designed to accommodate traditional teaching patterns in the self-contained
classroom. However, operable partitions between classrooms permit instant adaptation to team teaching. And,
since the systems approach allows relocation of partitions
and mechanical services, the school is adaptable to any
future changes in educational program.

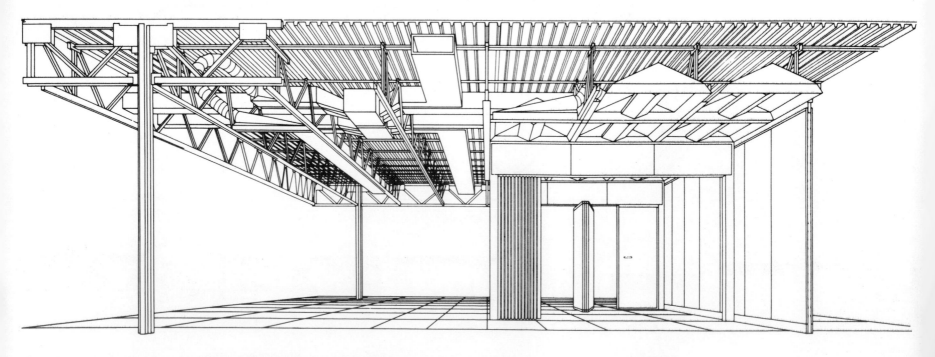

Coordinated structural, mechanical, ceiling-lighting, and partitioning features in a system of modular components

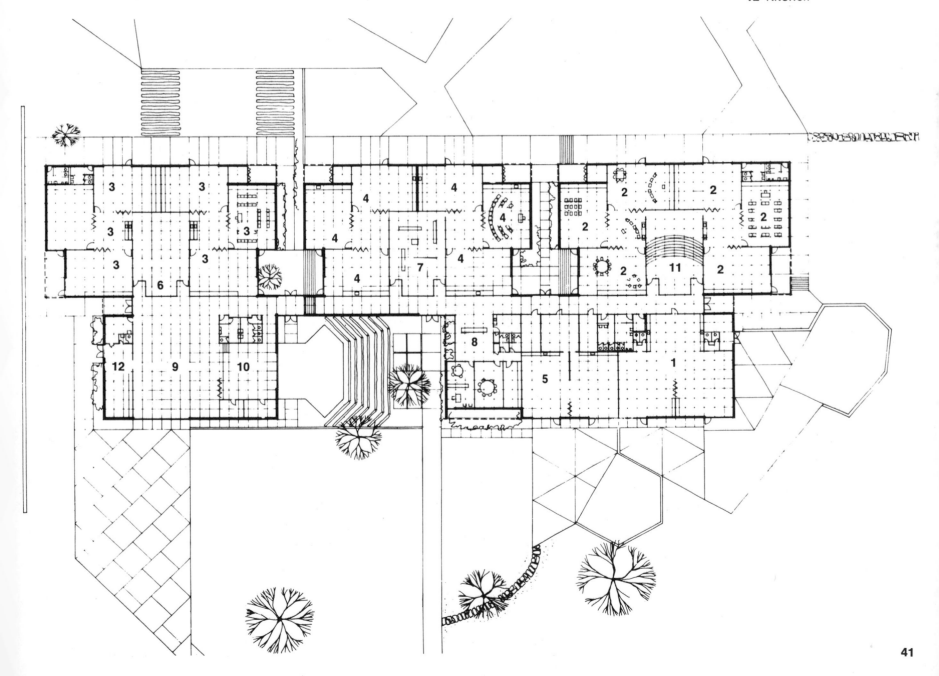

Floor plan:

1 Kindergarten
2 Primary classrooms
3 Intermediate classrooms
4 Classrooms
5 Special education
6 Laboratory
7 Library
8 Administration
9 Multi-purpose area
10 Music
11 Theater
12 Kitchen

18 Ravenwood Elementary School

Owner North Kansas City Board of Education, North Kansas City, Missouri

Superintendent Dr. Ruie B. Doolin

Principal James Thomas

Architects Kivett and Myers, Kansas City, Missouri

In charge James E. Arnold, Vice President, Educational Facilities

Mechanical-electrical engineers Bob Smith & Associates

Structural engineers Pfuhl & Stevson

Food service consultant W. Milt Santee

Occupancy September 1968

Capacity 400

Organization K-6

Project costs $550,000

Construction costs $425,987

Two six-classroom pods — one for primary and one for intermediate grades — characterize this open-plan, suburban elementary school. Planned around a "cooperative teaching" program, the plan allows the grouping and regrouping of pupils according to their immediate needs and progress in different subject areas. Isolated, special activity areas are provided for teaching situations requiring privacy or sound isolation.

Floor plan:
1 Kindergarten
2 Six-classroom unit
3 Teachers' planning
4 Special activity
5 Library
6 Administration
7 Health
8 Reception
9 Conference
10 Multi-purpose room
11 Kitchen
12 Teachers' lounge
13 Coats
14 Mechanical

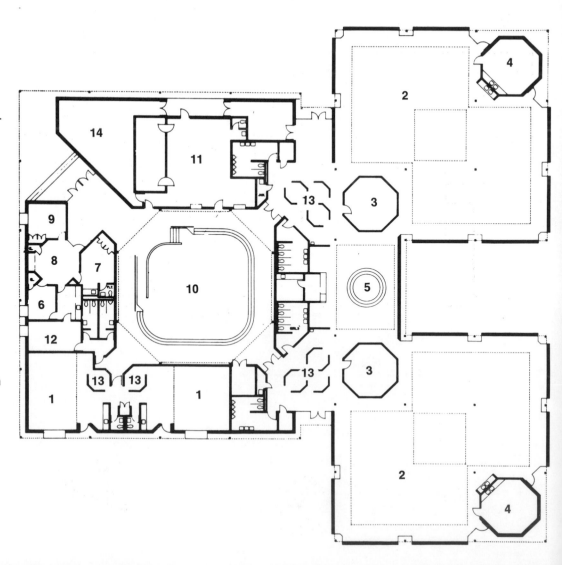

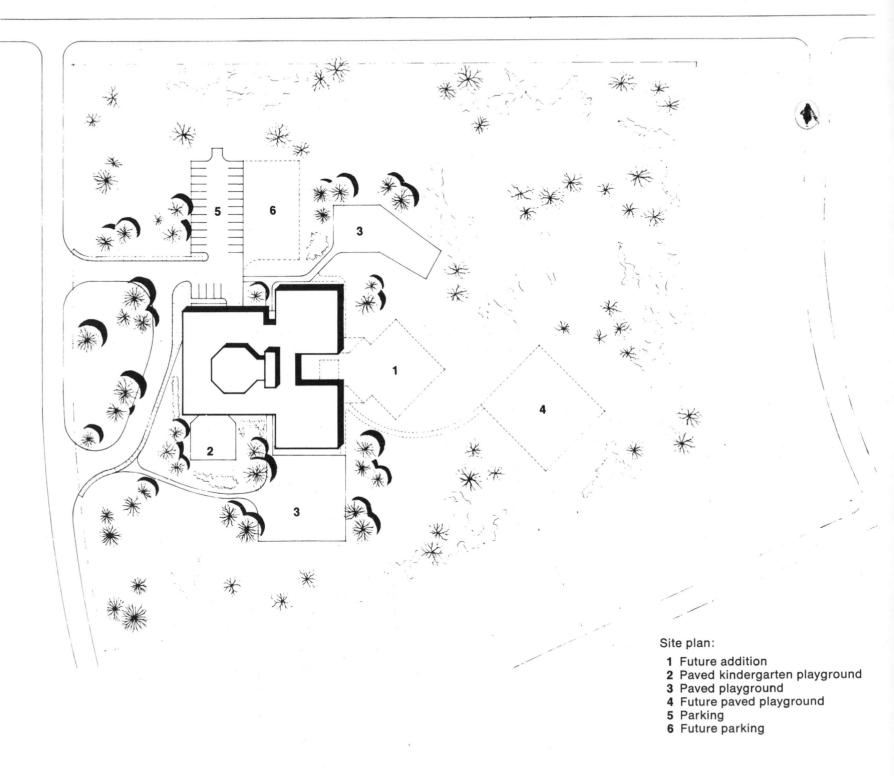

Site plan:

1 Future addition
2 Paved kindergarten playground
3 Paved playground
4 Future paved playground
5 Parking
6 Future parking

19 Comanche Elementary School

Owner Unified School District No. 512, Shawnee Mission, Kansas

Superintendent Dr. Arzell Ball

Principal Dr. James Owen

Architects Marshall & Brown of Kansas, Kansas City, Kansas

Project architect Robert B. Jarvis

Structural engineer F. A. Towner

Mechanical-electrical engineers Holloway, Perkins & Eisman

Occupancy September 1970

Capacity 400

Organization K-6

Construction costs $667,630

Pupils in this midwestern elementary school are divided by achievement and general age level into four communities of about 100 each. The communities are housed in their own open, group-work area, and supported by storage, special project, and teacher planning spaces. All four communities open directly into the school's library, or "learning center." The design is intended to facilitate a non-graded, continuous progress educational program.

Lower floor plan:

1 Teachers' workroom
2 Speech and conference
3 Administration
4 Health
5 Activity room
6 Music room
7 Dining
8 Kitchen
9 Lobby
10 Alcove
11 Mechanical
12 Fan room

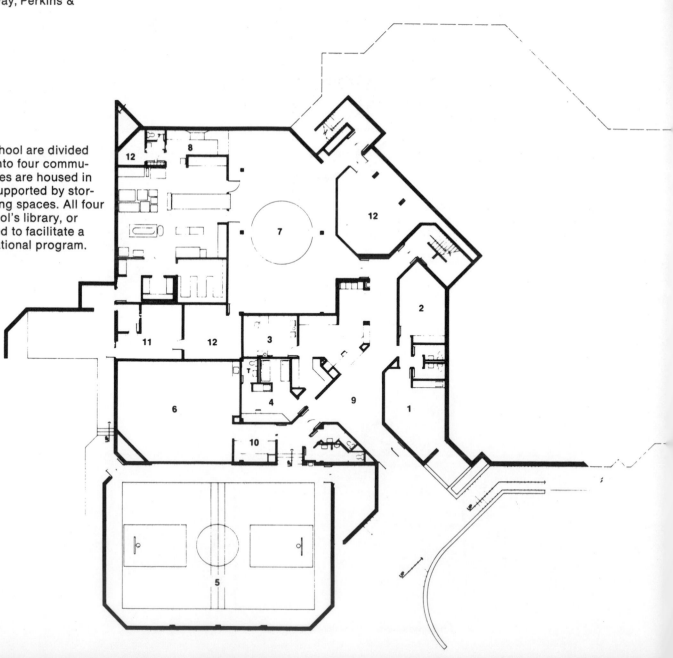

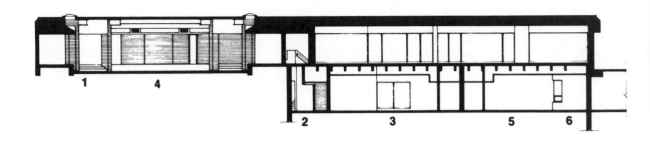

Cross section:

1 Project area
2 Speech
3 Administration
4 Community room
5 Fan room
6 Mechanical

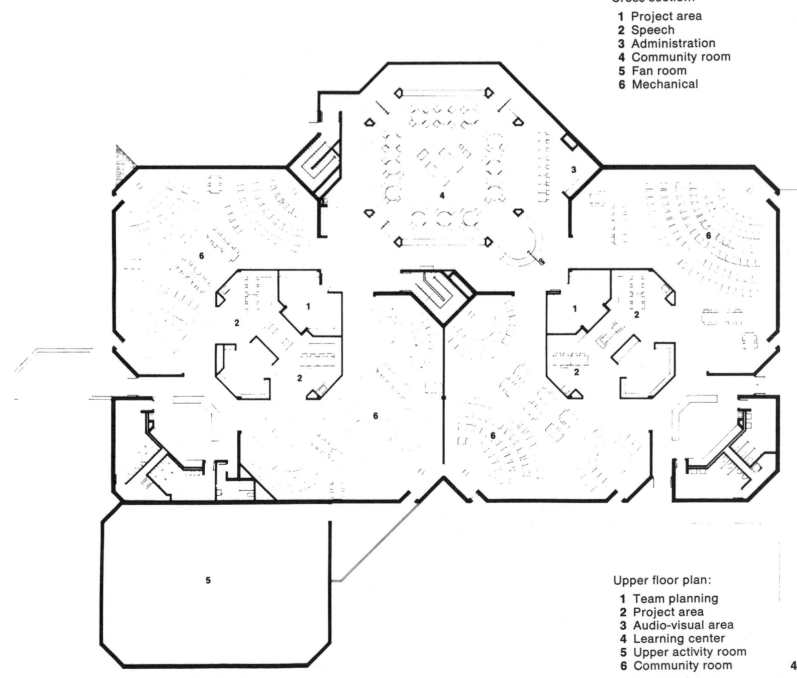

Upper floor plan:

1 Team planning
2 Project area
3 Audio-visual area
4 Learning center
5 Upper activity room
6 Community room

20 Shelton View School

Owner Northshore School District No. 417, State of Washington

Superintendent Julian Karp

Principal Dudley Halworth

Architects Harthorne, Hagen, Gross & Associates, Seattle, Washington

Project architect Cliff Gross

Mechanical engineer Stanley G. Webster

Electrical engineer Carl J. Radin

Occupancy January 1970

Capacity 600

Organization K-6

Project costs $906,500

Construction costs $752,500

A modern version of the campus plan, this school was designed to permit independent scheduling of different grade levels without disruption of other classes. Carpeted classrooms are grouped in pods for this purpose and are divided by operable partitions to permit variably sized instructional groupings. Each classroom building has six carpeted learning areas, an activities area, and a teacher-office meeting area.

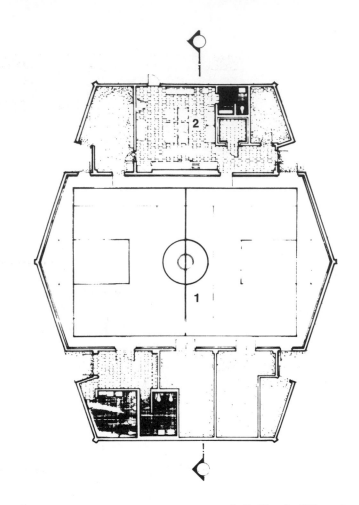

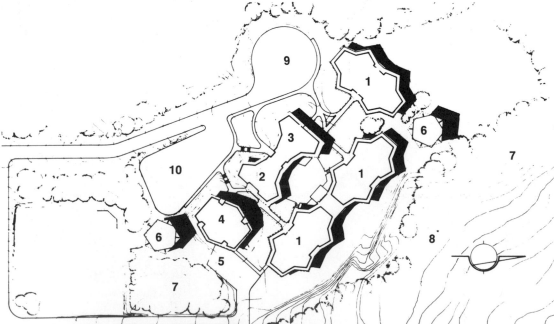

Activities building plan:

1 Multi-purpose room
2 Kitchen

Site plan:

1 Classrooms
2 Learning resource center
3 Administration
4 Multi-purpose room
5 Service
6 Covered play
7 Playground
8 Nature area
9 Bus loading
10 Parking

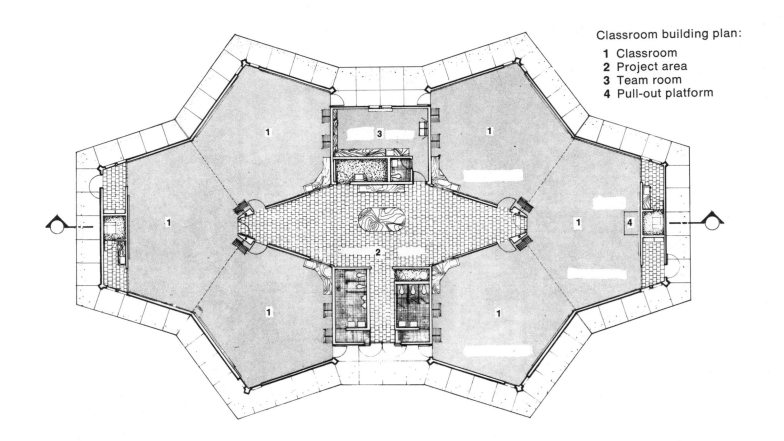

Classroom building plan:

1 Classroom
2 Project area
3 Team room
4 Pull-out platform

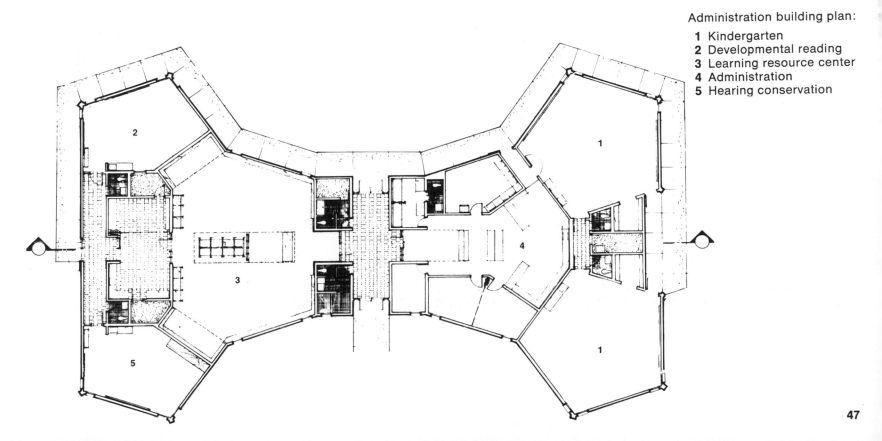

Administration building plan:

1 Kindergarten
2 Developmental reading
3 Learning resource center
4 Administration
5 Hearing conservation

21 Human Resources Center

Owner School District of the City of Pontiac, Pontiac, Michigan

Superintendent Dr. Dana P. Whitmer

Director Thor Petersen

Architects Urban Design Associates, Pittsburgh, Pennsylvania; O'Dell, Hewlett & Luckenbach, Inc., Pontiac, Michigan

Mechanical-electrical engineers Migdal, Layne & Sachs, Inc.

Structural engineer Joseph E. Spagnulo

Landscape architects Griswold, Winters & Swain

Occupancy September 1971

Capacity 2,200

Organization K-6

Construction costs $6,500,000

This urban educational/community service complex may be the harbinger of a future in which planners and architects will design communities rather than schools. The plan, developed with community participation and funded by local, state, and federal governments, includes such facilities as a theater for the performing arts, a 650-seat auditorium, a public restaurant, exhibition rooms, library, adult education facilities, and doctors' and dentists' offices, in addition to a modern, flexible educational plant. The complex also acts as a link between once-isolated neighborhoods of varying racial and economic makeup and as an "interface" between those neighborhoods and the city center.

Diagonal section:
1 Theater
2 Community fieldhouse
3 Cafetorium
4 Roof street

Community level plan:
1 Adult education
2 Library
3 Administration
4 Health
5 Parent-teacher counseling
6 Theater
7 Gymnasium-community fieldhouse
8 Cafetorium-Town Hall
9 Public restaurant
10 Community lounge
11 Community offices
12 Roof street

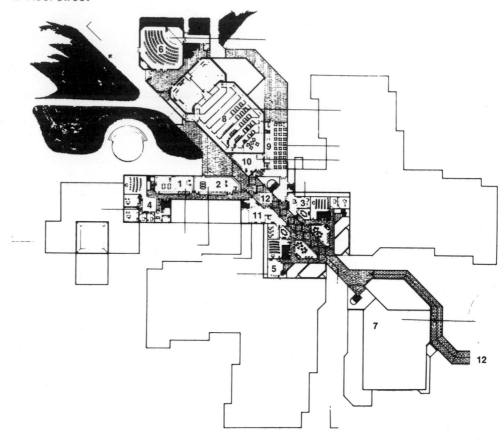

Longitudinal section:

1 Kindergarten
2 Learning center
3 Group teaching area
4 Teacher preparation
5 Mini-theater
6 Hideaway
7 Roof street

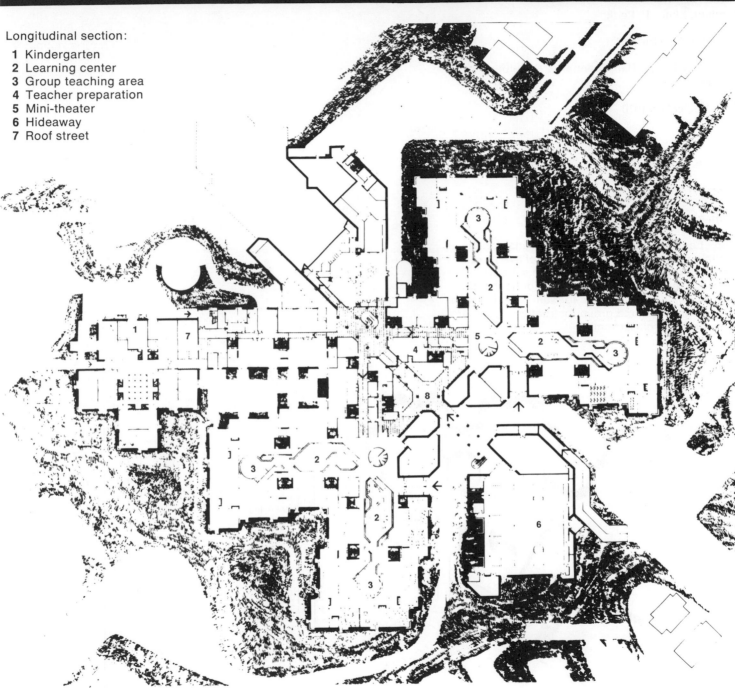

Student level plan:

1 Kindergarten
2 Learning center
3 Group teaching area
4 Teacher preparation
5 Mini-theater
6 Gymnasium-community fieldhouse
7 Hideaway
8 Roof street

22 Harris Hill Elementary School

Owner Board of Education, Penfield, New York

Superintendent Elmer F. Peck

Principal Richard J. Garland

Architects Parks, Morin, Hall, Brennan & Sattelberg, Rochester, New York

Occupancy November 1970

Capacity 600

Organization K-6

Project costs $1,696,000

Construction costs $1,309,900

The hexagon becomes the basic design for adaptability in this elementary school plan. Four clusters of five hexagonal classrooms each form the bulk of the school's instructional space. A hexagonal centrum forms the core of each cluster and provides space for seminars, independent studies or projects, and group instruction. There are no partitions between classrooms.

Site plan:

1 Elementary school
2 Parking

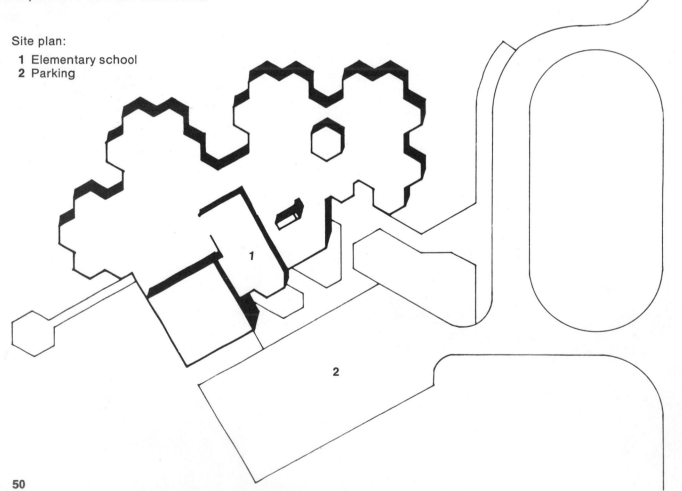

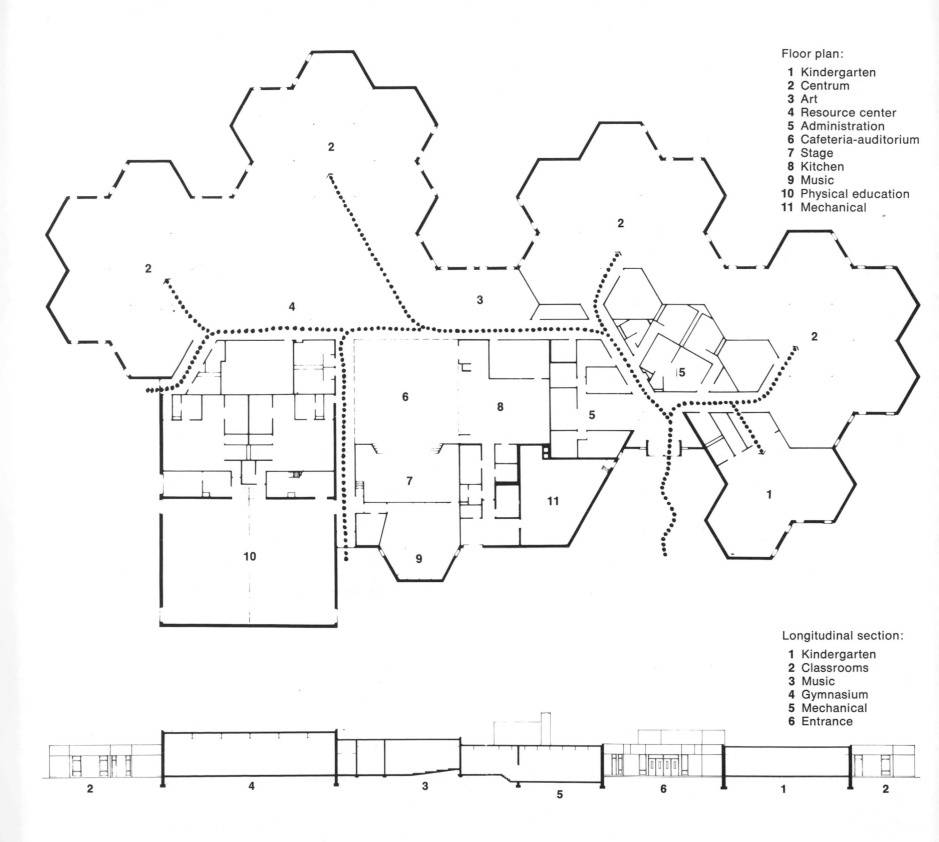

Floor plan:

1 Kindergarten
2 Centrum
3 Art
4 Resource center
5 Administration
6 Cafeteria-auditorium
7 Stage
8 Kitchen
9 Music
10 Physical education
11 Mechanical

Longitudinal section:

1 Kindergarten
2 Classrooms
3 Music
4 Gymnasium
5 Mechanical
6 Entrance

23 John F. Kennedy Elementary School

Owner Independent School District No. 29, Norman, Oklahoma

Superintendent Lester M. Reed

Principal Mrs. Fran Terry

Architects Kaighn Associates, Norman, Oklahoma

Structural engineer Sullivan Engineering

Mechanical-electrical engineers Determan & Schierman

Occupancy September 1968

Capacity 500

Organization 1-6

Project costs $689,957

Construction costs $570,114

An example of the school-without-walls approach to educational planning, this school houses virtually the entire instructional program for 500 pupils in one large, totally open room. The central resource center is flanked by two learning areas. In one, a team of teachers and aides conducts programs for the first three grades; a second team instructs upper graders in the other area. The building is air conditioned and, with the exception of the all-purpose dining area, fully carpeted.

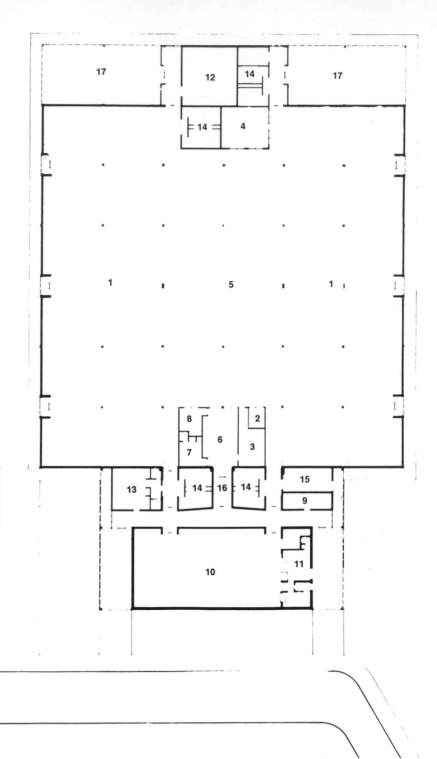

Floor plan:
1 Learning area
2 Special instruction
3 Teachers' workroom
4 Teachers' planning room
5 Resource center
6 Reception
7 Principal
8 Conference
9 Health
10 All-purpose area
11 Kitchen
12 Music room
13 Teachers' lounge
14 Toilet
15 Mechanical room
16 Display area
17 Covered play area

Cross section:
1 Learning area
2 Special instruction
3 Resource center
4 Conference room

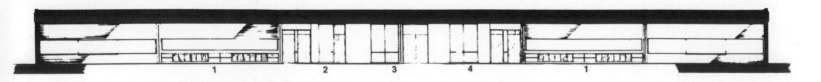

24 Lower School, Villa Duchesne

Owner Sisters of the Sacred Heart, St. Louis County, Missouri

Headmaster Robert Wray

Principal Sister Adele Caire

Architects William B. Ittner, Inc., St. Louis, Missouri

Project architect H. Curtis Ittner

Mechanical engineers Dan Siegel and Associates

Occupancy September 1969

Capacity 300

Organization 1-6

Construction costs $523,513

This five-building campus houses a newer lower school for a private institution in the St. Louis suburbs. Operable partitions are employed in the three classroom buildings to provide for some variety in instructional groupings.

Site plan:

1 Existing school buildings
2 Classroom pod
3 Administration building
4 Multi-purpose building

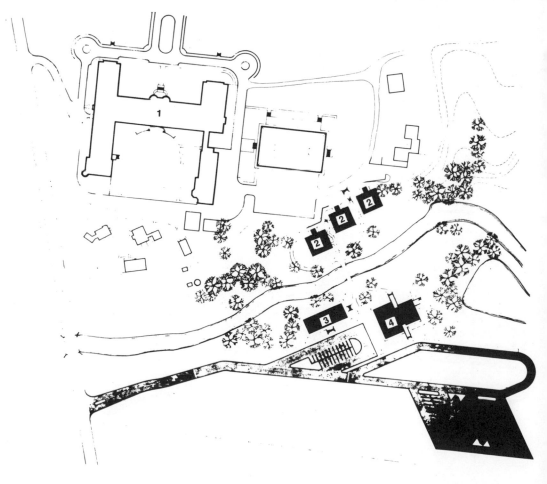

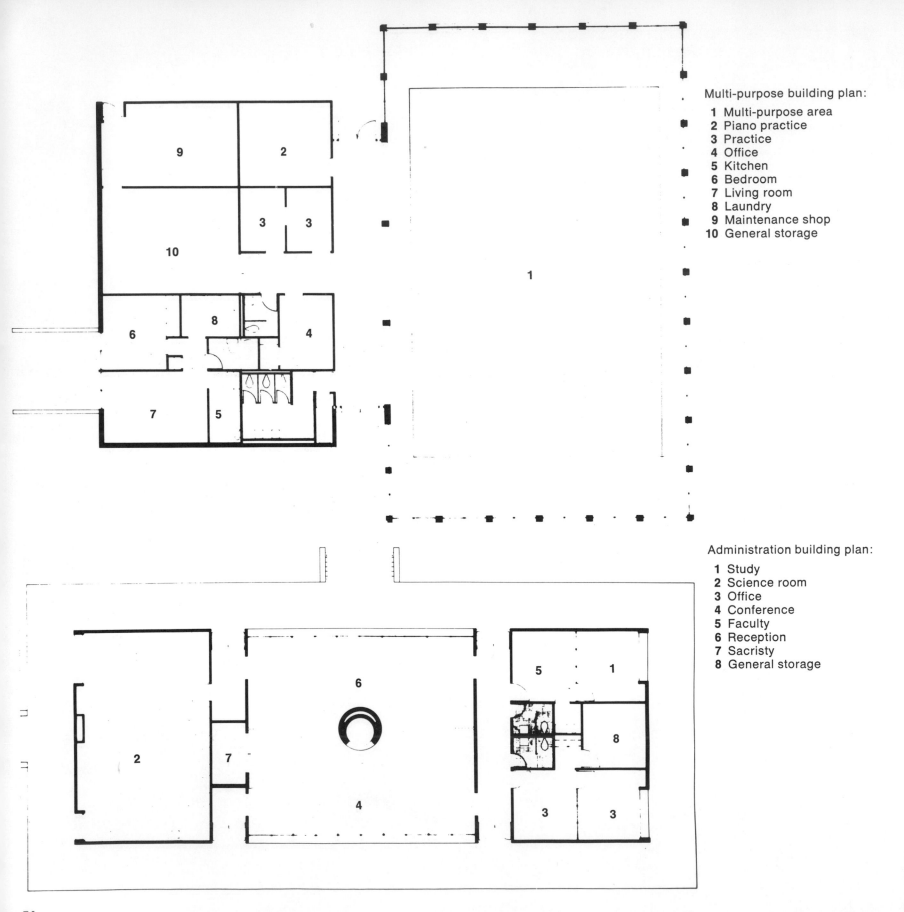

Multi-purpose building plan:

1 Multi-purpose area
2 Piano practice
3 Practice
4 Office
5 Kitchen
6 Bedroom
7 Living room
8 Laundry
9 Maintenance shop
10 General storage

Administration building plan:

1 Study
2 Science room
3 Office
4 Conference
5 Faculty
6 Reception
7 Sacristy
8 General storage

Lower floor plan:

1 Classroom
2 Activity area
3 Alcove

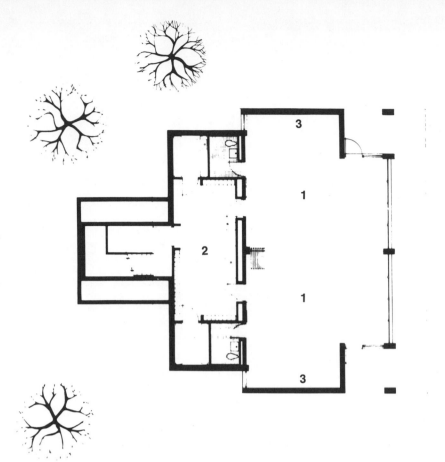

Upper floor plan:

1 Classroom
2 Activity area

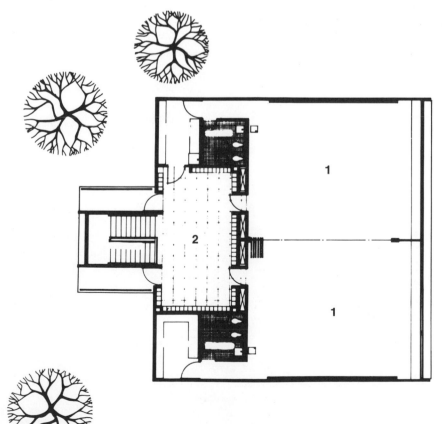

25 Bethany Elementary School

Owner Town of Bethany, Connecticut

Superintendent Franklin P. Plummer

Architects Steckler and Colavecchio Architects, Inc., Bloomfield, Connecticut

Landscape architects Allen W. Hixon, Jr. & Associates

Structural engineers Pfisterer, Tor and Associates

Mechanical engineers Hubbard, Lawless and Osborne Associates

Occupancy January 1970

Capacity 510

Organization 3-6

Project costs $1,300,000

Construction costs $952,600

Planned for a gradual transition from self-contained classroom instruction to more flexible, team-teaching methods, this upper elementary school's classrooms are clustered in groups of three, separated by operable partitions. A central common instructional area will be a resource center for the academic unit. The twelve-classroom unit provided in the first phase will be duplicated in a later phase.

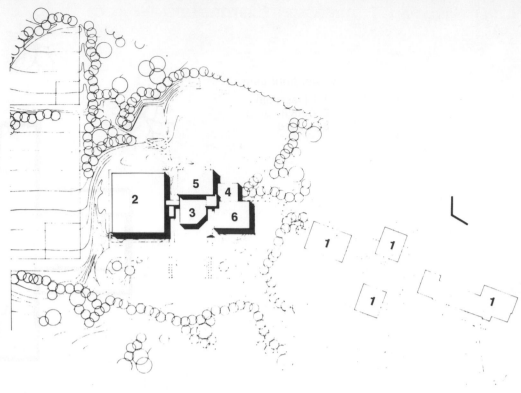

Site plan:
1 Existing facilities
2 Classroom wing
3 Library
4 Administration
5 Gymnasium
6 Cafetorium

Floor plan:
1 Classroom
2 Special education
3 Work
4 Library
5 Administration
6 Conference
7 Stage
8 Gymnasium
9 Cafetorium
10 Kitchen
11 Commons
12 Lounge
13 Lobby
14 Future offices
15 Future addition

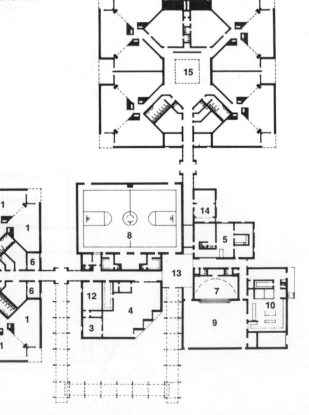

26 Warren T. Jackson Elementary School

Owner Atlanta Public Schools, Atlanta, Georgia

Superintendent John W. Letson

Principal Mrs. Marie Smart

Architect John W. Cherry, Atlanta, Georgia

Project architect John W. Cherry

Structural engineer Harry Hunter

Mechanical engineer J. W. Austin, Jr. & Associates, Inc.

Electrical engineer L. M. Reeves, Jr.

Occupancy November 1968

Capacity 660

Organization K-7

Project costs $806,000

Construction costs $722,030

Architectural interpretation of the new teaching patterns often is expressed in new and nonrectilinear shapes for the schoolhouse. In this case, space for team teaching was provided by clustering instructional areas in circular pods housing the equivalent of four classrooms each, plus a commons area, lavatories, and a teachers' workroom.

Lower floor plan:
1 Dining and auditorium
2 Kitchen
3 Serving area
4 Stage
5 Music room
6 Storage
7 Dining lobby
8 Mechanical equipment

Main floor plan:
1 Kindergarten
2 First grade
3 Second grade
4 Third grade
5 Fourth grade
6 Fifth grade
7 Sixth grade
8 Seventh grade
9 Teachers' workroom
10 Work
11 Resource center
12 Administration
13 Health
14 Conference
15 Commons
16 Classroom lobby
17 Foyer
18 Entrance lobby

Lower floor plan

Site plan

Main floor plan

27 Scott Elementary School Addition

Owner Atlanta Public Schools, Atlanta, Georgia

Superintendent John W. Letson

Principal Mrs. Birdie W. Robinson

Architect John W. Cherry, Atlanta, Georgia

Structural engineer Harry Hunter

Mechanical engineer J. W. Austin, Jr. & Associates, Inc.

Electrical engineer Newman-Hibble & Associates

Landscape architect Joe W. Arnold Company

Occupancy October 1970

Capacity 400

Organization K-7

Project costs $545,700

Construction costs $498,500

Team-teaching capacity was added to this school through an addition that provided two open instructional areas, in addition to needed expansion of dining and library facilities. Each open pod includes four classrooms plus a shared commons area. The pods also boast offices and conference rooms for teacher planning, teacher-parent conferences, independent study, and seminars. The addition is located in front of the old building to give the school a new image.

Site plan:
1 Elementary school
2 School addition

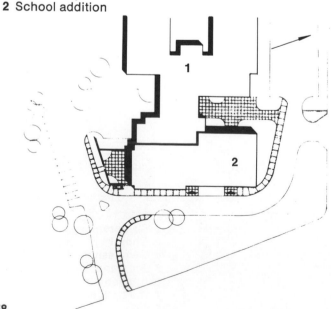

Main floor plan:
1 Classroom
2 Office
3 Conference
4 Cafetorium
5 Gallery
6 Stage
7 Kitchen
8 Dishwasher
9 Commons
10 Wet area
11 Mechanical
12 Electrical

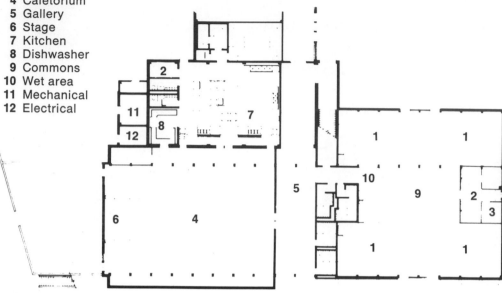

Second floor plan:
1 Classroom
2 Library
3 Story telling
4 Office and workroom
5 Conference
6 Commons
7 Wet area
8 Balcony

28 Hammond Elementary/Middle School

Owner Board of Education, Howard County, Maryland

Superintendent M. Thomas Goedeke

Architects Sandlass Craycroft & Verkerke, Baltimore, Maryland

Occupancy September 1971

Capacity 600 (elementary), 800 (middle)

Organization K-5, 6-8

Project costs $3,000,000

Construction costs $2,240,000

Originally contemplated as separate buildings, these two schools ultimately were combined for reasons of economy, efficiency, and greater educational continuity and opportunity. While the schools share facilities in the core and the physical education wing, each is designed to retain its identity. Both feature open and flexible team-teaching spaces, a separate instructional materials center, and liberal provisions for team planning and projects.

Main floor plan:
1 Kindergarten
2 Primary
3 Learning center
4 Team project room
5 Project area
6 Science
7 Language laboratory
8 Art
9 Arts-crafts
10 Metal-wood shop
11 Foods
12 Clothing
13 Elementary instruction materials center

14 Middle instructional materials center
15 Administration and health
16 Conference
17 Special purpose
18 Music
19 Gymnasium
20 Orchestra
21 Choral
22 Teachers' workroom, planning, lounge
23 Gallery
24 Open court

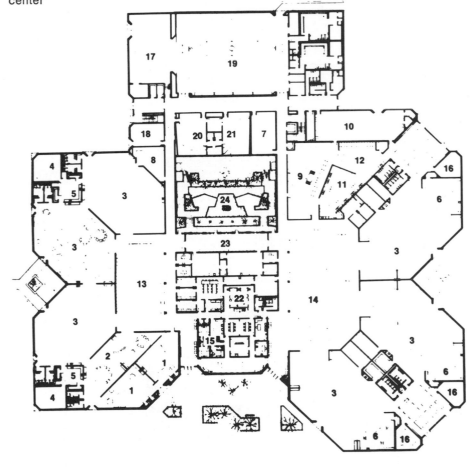

Lower level plan:
1 Multi-purpose room
2 Cafeteria
3 Kitchen

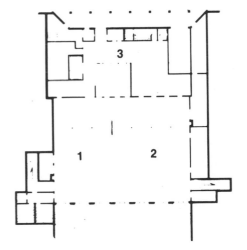

Longitudinal section:
1 Media
2 Conference
3 Choral
4 Gymnasium
5 Cafeteria
6 Kitchen
7 Reception
8 Court

29 Fox Lane Middle School

Owner Bedford School District No. 2, Bedford, New York

Superintendent Charles O. Richter (during planning and design)

Architects The Architects Collaborative, Cambridge, Massachusetts

Principals-in-charge John C. Harkness, Sarah P. Harkness

Structural engineers Souza & True

Mechanical engineers Reardon & Turner

Electrical engineers Maguire Engineering

Occupancy September 1966

Capacity 1,000

Organization 6-8

Project costs $3,912,985

Construction costs $2,965,824

One of the earliest projects to be designed specifically to house the middle-school concept, this building, according to an early planning committee, is "suited to the peculiar requirements of children in the 'middle' of their public school life" and planned for well-thought-out combinations of teaching and learning groups. Library and study areas are liberally equipped with individual study carrels.

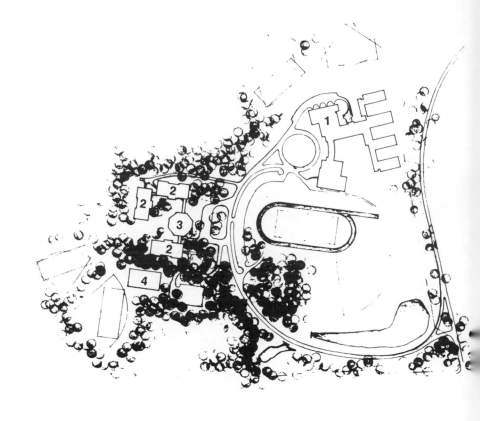

Site plan:

1 Existing school
2 Academic House
3 Unified arts center
4 Physical education

Upper level:

1 Classroom
2 Lecture room
3 Study area
4 Sub-library
5 Serving area

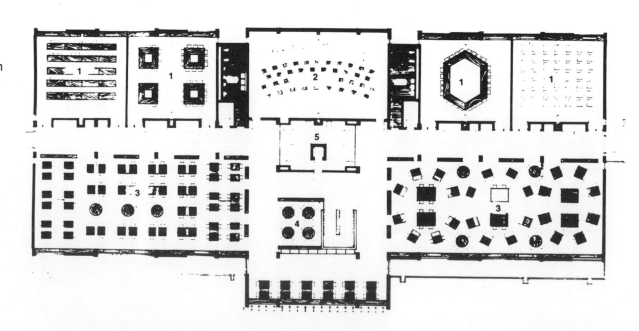

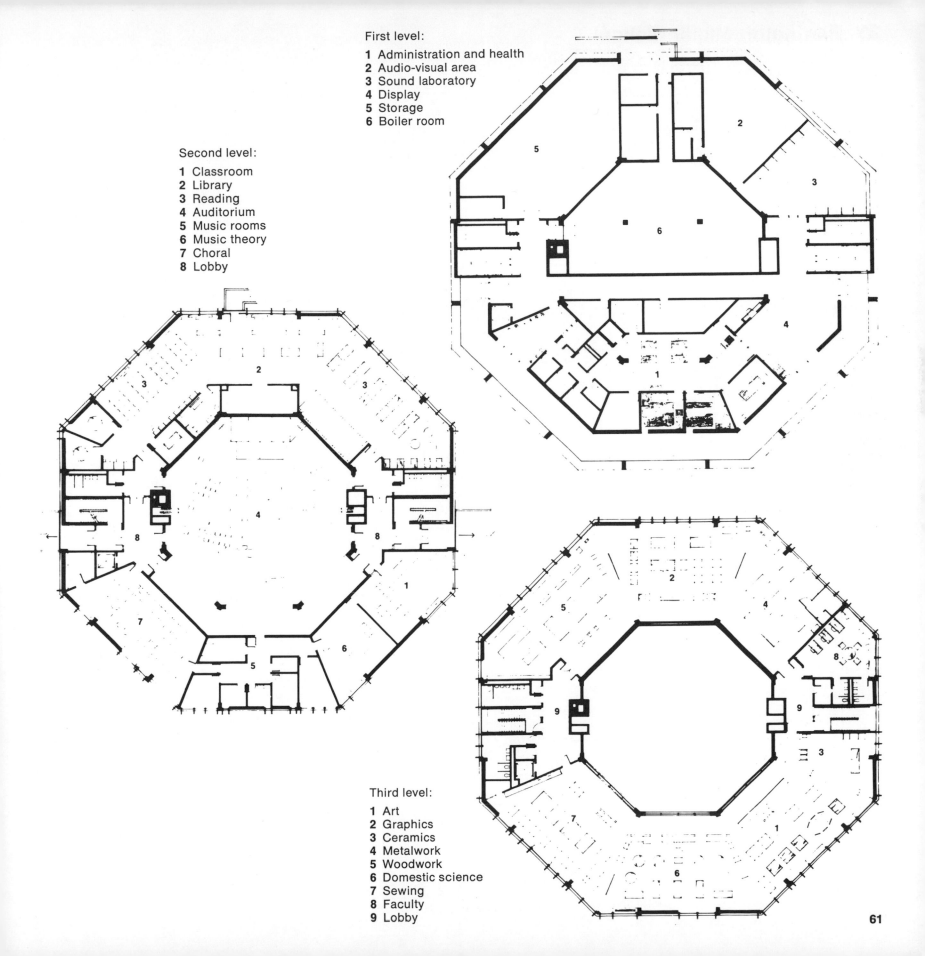

First level:

1 Administration and health
2 Audio-visual area
3 Sound laboratory
4 Display
5 Storage
6 Boiler room

Second level:

1 Classroom
2 Library
3 Reading
4 Auditorium
5 Music rooms
6 Music theory
7 Choral
8 Lobby

Third level:

1 Art
2 Graphics
3 Ceramics
4 Metalwork
5 Woodwork
6 Domestic science
7 Sewing
8 Faculty
9 Lobby

30 Barrington Middle School

Owner Community School District No. 4, Barrington, Illinois

Superintendent Robert Finley (during planning)

Principal Walter Pagels

Architects Cone & Dornbusch, Chicago, Illinois

Project architect Spencer B. Cone

Mechanical and structural engineers The Engineers Collaborative

Occupancy Fall 1965

Capacity 1,200

Organization 6-8

Projection costs $1,559,000

Construction costs $1,200,000

The oldest of the projects in this book, the Barrington Middle School is included as a landmark: it was the first American schoolhouse to be built with modular, prefabricated components. The components were developed by industry under the School Construction Systems Development Projects (SCSD) in California. Handed an educational program calling for a non-graded, completely flexible middle school employing team teaching, the architects seized on the SCSD system as ideal, and employed it before any of the SCSD project schools in California were ready for construction. The open-classroom layout shown in the floor plans since has been modified by the simple expedient of relocating and adding demountable partitions.

First floor plan:

1 Classroom unit
2 Science study court
3 Art
4 Shop
5 Home economics
6 Drafting
7 Learning center
8 Stage
9 Band
10 Vocal
11 Physical education
12 Dining and creative programing
13 Kitchen
14 Faculty
15 Planetarium
16 Art terrace
17 Band terrace
18 Study court
19 Service court

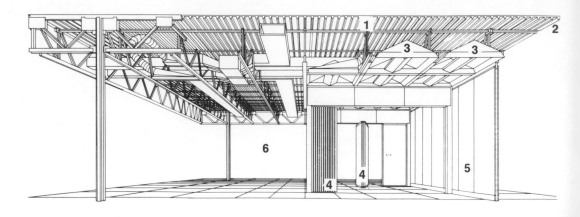

SCSD system component:

1 Truss-deck system
2 Integrated sandwich
3 Ceiling-lighting coffer
4 Operable partition
5 Demountable partition
6 Clear span

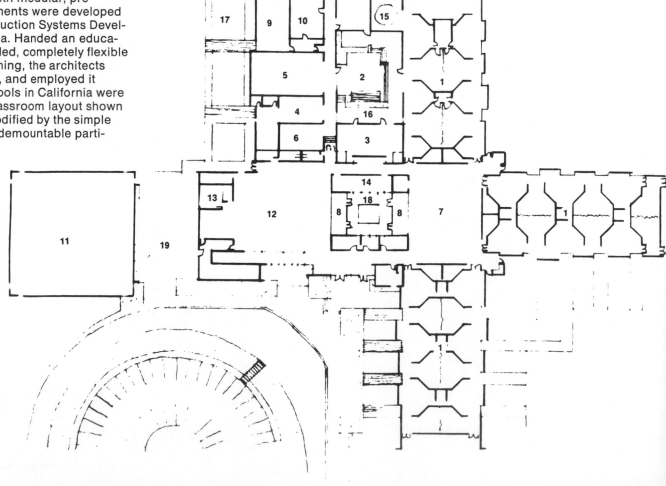

31 Chardon Middle School

Owner Chardon Local School District, Chardon, Ohio

Superintendent Walter S. Smith

Principal Kenneth Lampman

Architects Dela Motte, Larson, Nassau & Associates, Cleveland, Ohio

Occupancy 1967

Capacity 600

Organization 6-8

Project costs $937,200

Construction costs $799,194

Designed with the help of the Educational Research Council of Greater Cleveland, this plan provides for a gradual transition from the self-contained, single-teacher classroom found in local elementary schools to the multi-teacher, departmentalized program in the high schools. Accordingly, the building contains both traditional classrooms and large-group lecture halls. A sizable library is provided for pupils taking on the responsibility of independent study.

First floor plan:
1 Classroom
2 Teachers' planning
3 Library
4 Administration and health

Longitudinal section:
1 First floor
2 Classroom
3 Lecture
4 Science room
5 Library
6 Gymnasium
7 Gymnasium storage
8 Cafeteria
9 Storage

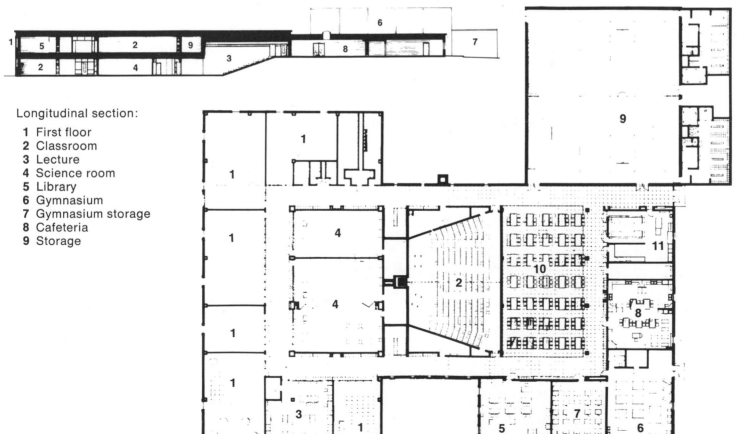

Second floor -
ground floor plan:
1 Classroom
2 Lecture room
3 Teachers' planning
4 Science room
5 Art room
6 Shop
7 Mechanical drawing
8 Home economics
9 Gymnasium
10 Cafeteria
11 Kitchen

32 A New Junior High School

Owner Festus R-VI School District, Festus, Missouri

Superintendent Ralph B. Tynes

Architects William B. Ittner, Inc., St. Louis, Missouri

Structural engineers Heinicke & Theiss

Occupancy September 1971

Capacity 400

Organization 7-8

Construction costs $829,581

Planned around the self-contained classroom, this school nevertheless involves some intriguing departures from past practice. Most interesting is the use of the carpeted corridors adjacent to the library to provide carrel-equipped independent study space. While windows are located at two corners of most classrooms, the emphasis is on their use to provide natural light rather than a view of the outdoors.

Site plan:

1 Existing building
2 Future addition
3 Bus loading
4 Parking

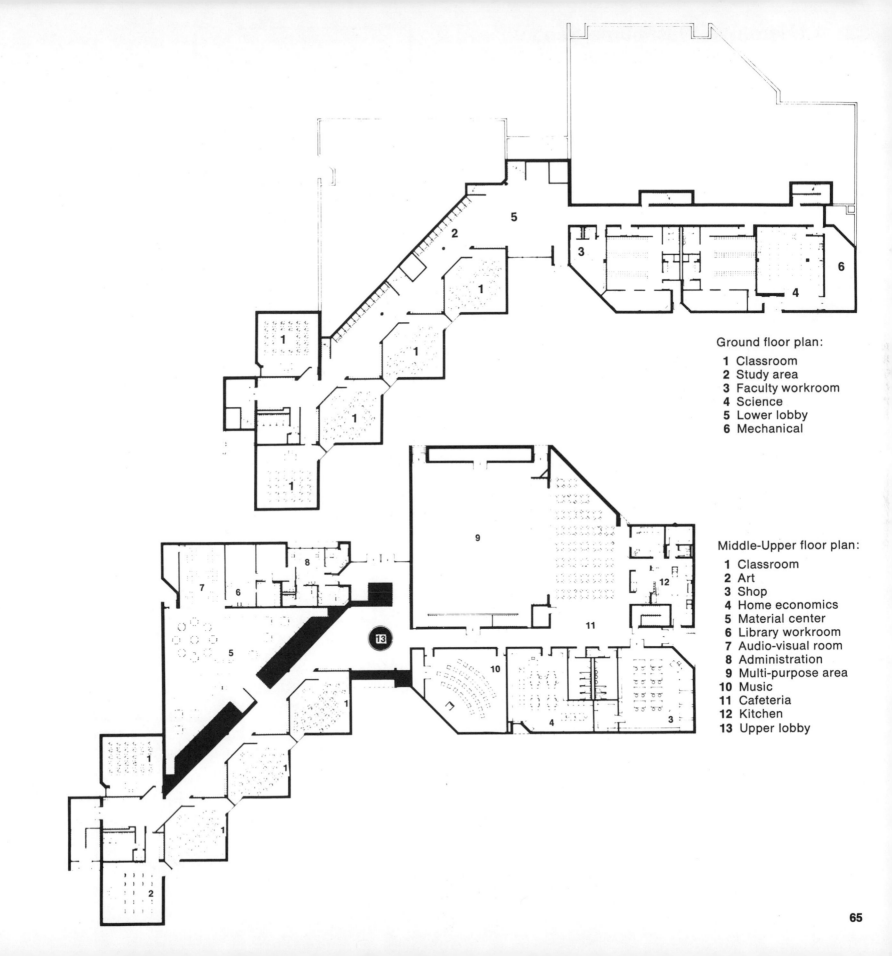

Ground floor plan:

1 Classroom
2 Study area
3 Faculty workroom
4 Science
5 Lower lobby
6 Mechanical

Middle-Upper floor plan:

1 Classroom
2 Art
3 Shop
4 Home economics
5 Material center
6 Library workroom
7 Audio-visual room
8 Administration
9 Multi-purpose area
10 Music
11 Cafeteria
12 Kitchen
13 Upper lobby

33 Carleton W. Washburne School

Owner Winnetka Public Schools, Winnetka, Illinois

Superintendent Dr. Robert Filbin

Principal Joe A. Richardson

Architects The Perkins & Will Partnership, Chicago, Illinois

Project architect Charles William Brubaker

Engineers P&W Engineers, Inc.

Theater consultant James Hull Miller

Landscaping Wallace G. Atkinson

Occupancy 1969

Capacity 600 (first phase), 900 (ultimate)

Organization 7-8

Construction costs $2,500,000

This plan for a suburban middle school provides for two academic units (a third is to be added later) grouped around a hub containing such facilities as a theater, a library, and a learning laboratory. The conventional classroom remains as the basic element in the academic units, but operable partitions between classrooms permit variable groupings. And, since most interior partitions are non-load-bearing, the units can be converted to a fully open plan should future programs require it.

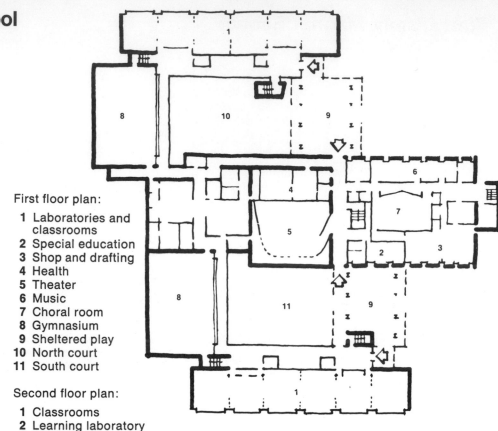

First floor plan:
1 Laboratories and classrooms
2 Special education
3 Shop and drafting
4 Health
5 Theater
6 Music
7 Choral room
8 Gymnasium
9 Sheltered play
10 North court
11 South court

Second floor plan:
1 Classrooms
2 Learning laboratory
3 Library resource center
4 Office
5 Theater
6 Multi-purpose area
7 Upper Gymnasium
8 North court
9 South court

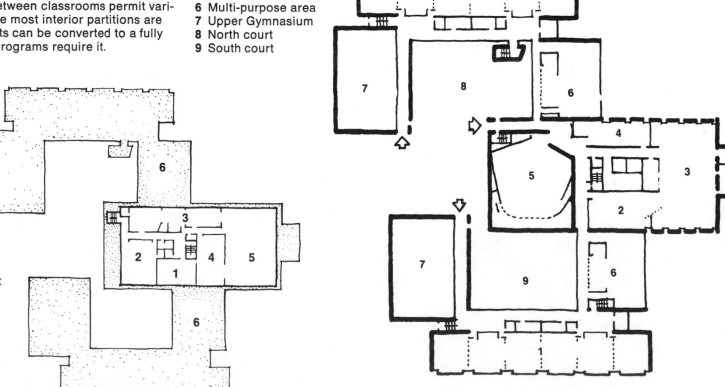

Third floor plan:
1 Typing
2 Art
3 TV studio-graphic arts
4 Home economics
5 Mechanical equipment
6 Roof

34 Walt Disney Magnet School

Owner Public Building Commission of Chicago (to be leased to Chicago Public Schools) Chicago, Illinois

Superintendent Dr. James F. Redmond

Principal Dr. Lorraine LaVigne

Architects The Perkins & Will Partnership, Chicago, Illinois

Project architect Morton Hartman

Mechanical-electrical engineers Kralovec & Best

Structural engineers P&W Engineers, Inc.

Occupancy September 1972

Capacity 1,800 (plus 600 visiting students from other schools)

Organization Preschool-9 in three age groups: 3-7, 7-11, 11-14

Project costs $12,000,000

Construction costs $9,000,000

Chicago proposes to build a series of "magnet" schools, attracting students from all parts of the city and not from the immediate neighborhood. Each magnet school will be different in program, character, age range, and size, and all will be frankly experimental. The first, the Walt Disney School, will emphasize the communication arts. Also of interest is the use of rooftops to provide recreation space on a tight, urban site.

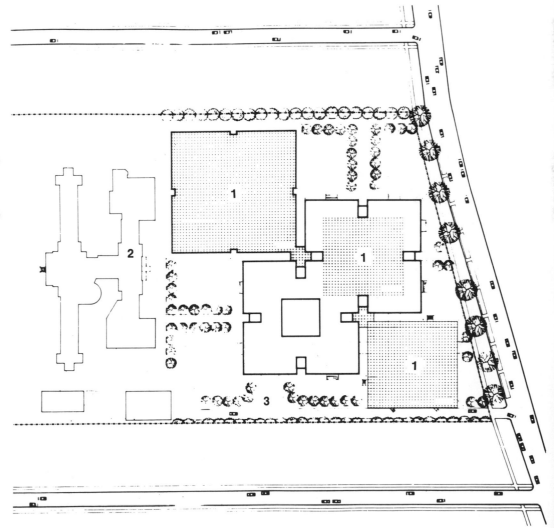

Site plan:

1 Outdoor play and recreation area
2 Existing hospital
3 Service drive

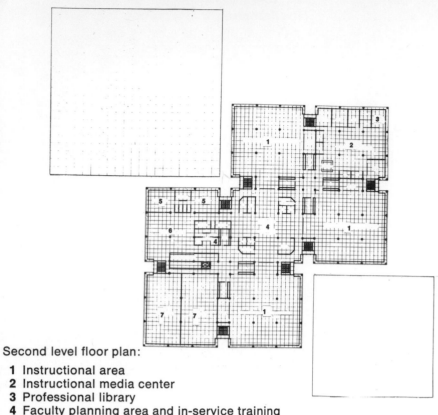

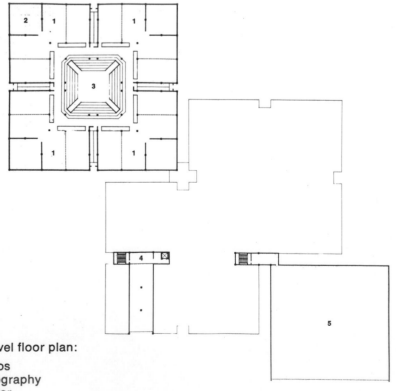

Second level floor plan:

1 Instructional area
2 Instructional media center
3 Professional library
4 Faculty planning area and in-service training
5 Music
6 Dining
7 Physical education below

First level floor plan:

1 Instructional
2 Visual arts
3 Display studio
4 Central administration
5 Health
6 Faculty planning area
7 Workroom
8 Physical education
9 Dining
10 Kitchen
11 Switch gear
12 Open space
13 Parking below
14 Plaza

Lower level floor plan:

1 Studios
2 Photography
3 Theater
4 Dock
5 Parking

Third level floor plan:

1 Instructional area
2 Science
3 Math
4 Art
5 Faculty planning area and in-service training
6 Physical education
7 Dining

35 Plymouth Junior High School

Owner Plymouth Township School District Authority, Colonial School District, Plymouth Township, Pennsylvania

Superintendent Dr. Gerald G. Hottenstein

Principal James I. Graham

Architects Anthony T. Rienzi & Associates, Philadelphia, Pennsylvania

Structural engineers Schulcz and Padlasky

Mechanical engineers Robert G. Werden & Associates

Occupancy October 1968

Capacity 1,200

Organization 7-9

Project costs $5,008,517

Construction costs $4,071,936

Triangular classrooms, basically self-contained, predominate in this junior high school. Operable partitions are employed in several locations to accommodate large-group instruction, which also is possible in the school auditorium. Isolation of physical education facilities, cafeteria, and library in separate building elements, which permits their use outside school hours, represents an interesting solution to the public-use problem.

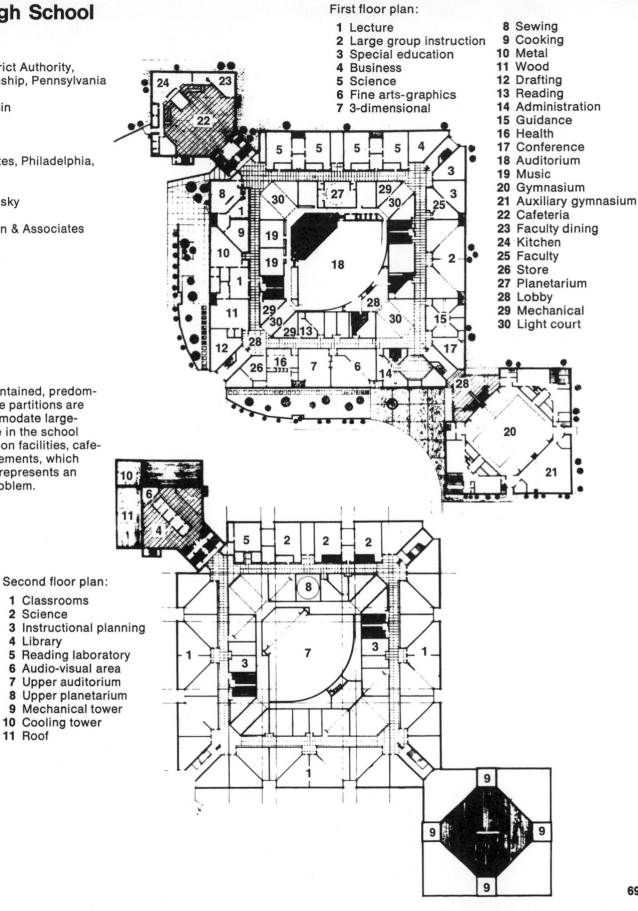

First floor plan:
1 Lecture
2 Large group instruction
3 Special education
4 Business
5 Science
6 Fine arts-graphics
7 3-dimensional
8 Sewing
9 Cooking
10 Metal
11 Wood
12 Drafting
13 Reading
14 Administration
15 Guidance
16 Health
17 Conference
18 Auditorium
19 Music
20 Gymnasium
21 Auxiliary gymnasium
22 Cafeteria
23 Faculty dining
24 Kitchen
25 Faculty
26 Store
27 Planetarium
28 Lobby
29 Mechanical
30 Light court

Second floor plan:
1 Classrooms
2 Science
3 Instructional planning
4 Library
5 Reading laboratory
6 Audio-visual area
7 Upper auditorium
8 Upper planetarium
9 Mechanical tower
10 Cooling tower
11 Roof

36 Evergreen Junior High School

Owner Jefferson County School District R-1, Colorado

Superintendent Dr. W. Del Walker

Principal Richard Frost

Architects Lamar Kelsey & Associates, Colorado Springs, Colorado

Structural engineer John E. Bunts

Mechanical-electrical engineers Swanson-Rink & Associates

Occupancy September 1969

Capacity 800

Organization 7-9

Construction costs $1,113,756

Three strong commitments characterize this junior high school design. The first is a commitment to the school's setting in rolling, wooded Colorado countryside, implemented by careful siting and the imaginative use of exterior materials and finishes. Another is the conclusion that some educational functions — art, physical education, music, homemaking — are relatively fixed in nature and that they can be housed in relatively inflexible quarters divided by masonry partitions. Last is that the balance of the educational process is in flux and that, through open planning and the use of demountable partitions and flexible ceiling and air-handling systems, adaptability must be provided.

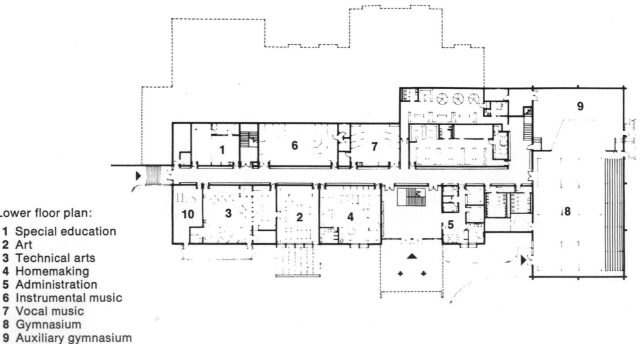

Lower floor plan:
1 Special education
2 Art
3 Technical arts
4 Homemaking
5 Administration
6 Instrumental music
7 Vocal music
8 Gymnasium
9 Auxiliary gymnasium
10 Mechanical

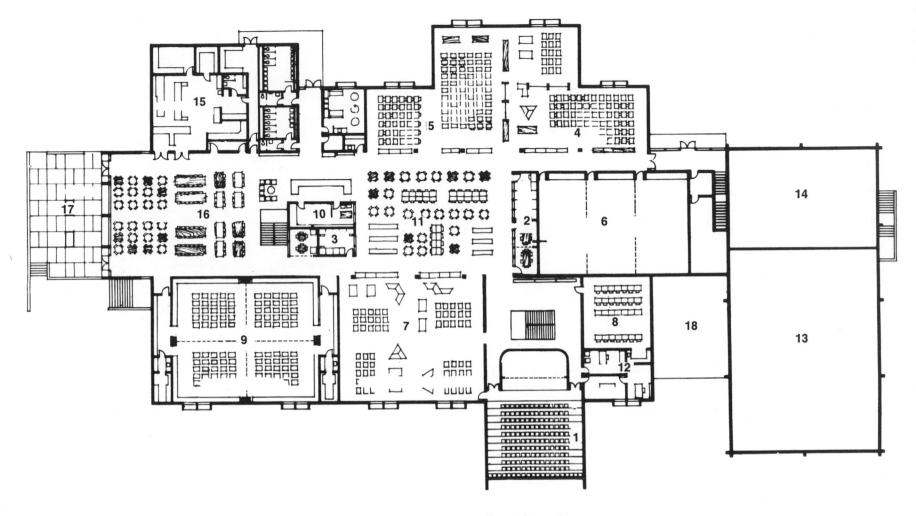

Upper floor plan:

1 Lecture
2 Seminar
3 Teachers' work
4 Language arts
5 Social studies
6 Foreign language
7 Mathematics
8 Typing
9 Science
10 Audio-visual
11 Instructional materials center
12 Office
13 Upper gymnasium
14 Upper auxiliary gymnasium
15 Kitchen
16 Student center
17 Patio
18 Roof

37 Junior High School

Owner Eaton Rapids Public Schools, Eaton Rapids, Michigan

Superintendent W. Carl Holbrook

Architects Louis C. Kingscott & Associates, Inc., Kalamazoo, Michigan

Project architect Brooks H. Godfrey

Occupancy September 1970

Capacity 950

Organization 7-9

Project costs $2,945,486

Construction costs $2,458,500

In this junior high school plan, the standard instructional unit is a departmental cluster of six classrooms, plus seminar and teacher planning rooms. In the science unit, four classrooms are equipped for lecture-demonstration and two as student laboratories. Operable partitions permit use of the classroom in a self-contained format or, when open, for variable groupings. They also are employed in the cafeteria to convert it for use as a large-group instruction room.

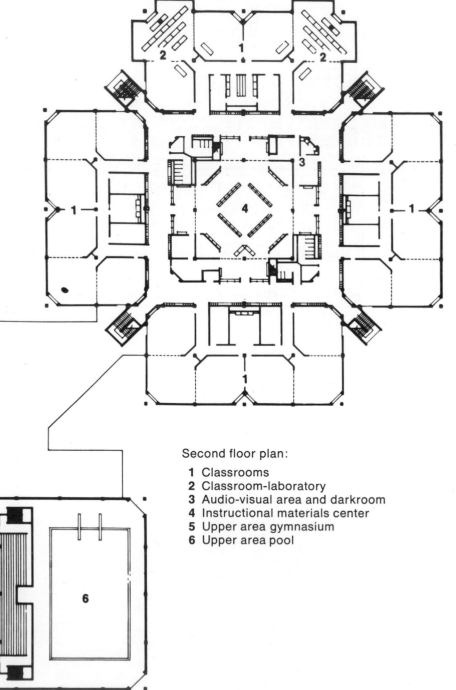

Second floor plan:

1 Classrooms
2 Classroom-laboratory
3 Audio-visual area and darkroom
4 Instructional materials center
5 Upper area gymnasium
6 Upper area pool

First floor plan:

1 Classroom
2 Special education
3 Art room
4 Drafting
5 Wood shop
6 Metal shop
7 Homemaking
8 Office and library
9 Administration and health
10 Band and vocal room
11 Gymnasium
12 Pool
13 Boys' locker room and shower
14 Girls' locker room and shower
15 Large group instruction and cafeteria
16 Teachers' lounge
17 Bookstore
18 Lobby
19 Boiler room

38 Manse Road Senior Public School

Owner Scarborough Board of Education, Scarborough, Ontario, Canada

Superintendent D. S. Taylor

Architects Craig Zeidler Strong, Toronto, Ontario, Canada

Partner-in-charge W. A. Strong

Project architect Ralph D. Stukator

Mechanical-electrical engineers W. Hardy Craig and Associates

Structural engineers John Maryon & Partners

Occupancy September 1970

Capacity 665

Organization 7-9

Construction costs $1,338,106, Canadian currency

The three-classroom clusters of instructional space here represent an attempt to provide compact, intimate teaching units within an open plan. A variety of seating arrangements that keep the students' backs to the corridor are possible within the classroom areas. The cafeteria, teamteaching area, and instrumental and vocal music spaces combine to create an auditorium for performances and parent-teacher meetings.

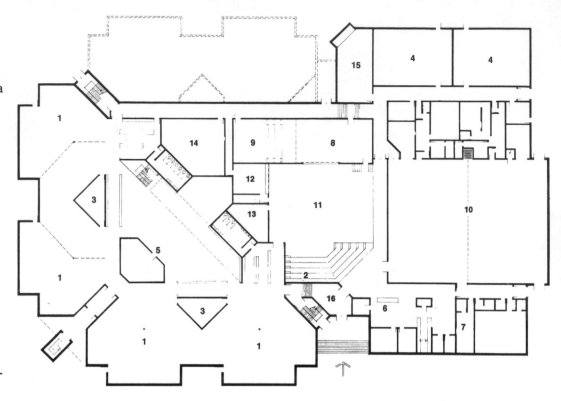

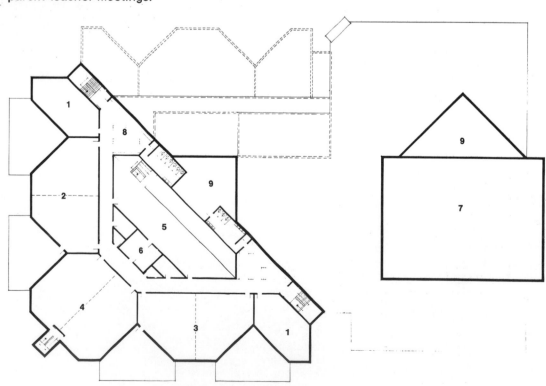

First floor plan:

1 Classroom cluster
2 Team teaching
3 Teacher preparation
4 Industrial arts
5 Resource center
6 Administration
7 Health
8 Stage - instrumental music
9 Vocal music
10 Double gymnasium
11 Cafeteria
12 Kitchen area
13 Storage
14 Mechanical
15 Boiler room
16 Vestibule

Second floor plan:

1 French
2 Science
3 Art
4 Home economics
5 Audio-visual area
6 Conference
7 Upper gymnasium
8 Lockers
9 Mechanical

39 Thomas Jefferson Junior High School and Community Center

Owner Arlington County, Virginia

Superintendent Dr. Robert L. Chisholm

Principal Joseph Macekura

Architects Vosbeck Vosbeck Kendrick Redinger, Alexandria, Virginia

Occupancy September 1972

Capacity 1,400

Organization 7-9

Project costs $6,200,000

Construction costs $5,400,000

A "controlled environment facility," a completely enclosed, 68,000-square foot, air conditioned space that provides recreational facilities for both school and community, is the outstanding feature of this junior high school plan. Its 30-foot ceiling height and clear spans of 160 by 385 feet allow for a variety of activities, from school basketball games to community art shows. Instructional facilities are characterized by a school-within-a-school concept, an open plan within each of three little schools, and an auditorium divisible by operable partitions into four large-group lecture halls.

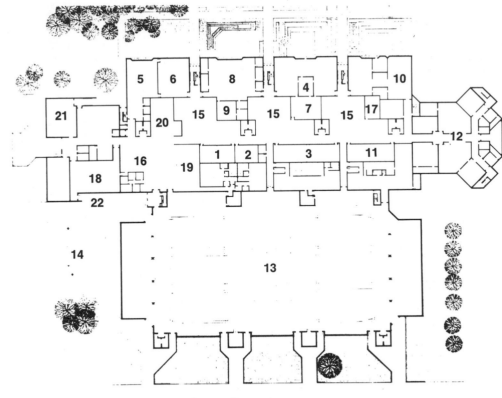

Lower floor plan:

1 Classroom
2 Business
3 Typing
4 Art
5 Applied arts
6 Industrial arts
7 Art laboratory
8 Industrial arts laboratory
9 Electrical laboratory
10 Home economics
11 Health
12 Music
13 Controlled environment facility
14 Special activities
15 Dining commons
16 Canteen
17 Teachers' dining
18 Kitchen
19 Game room
20 Club room
21 Mechanical
22 Recreation entrance

Upper floor plan:

1 School A
2 School B
3 School C
4 Staff and seminar area
5 Special education
6 Speech
7 Foreign language
8 Science laboratory
9 Library
10 Administration
11 Auditorium
12 Upper portion controlled environment facility
13 Lobby

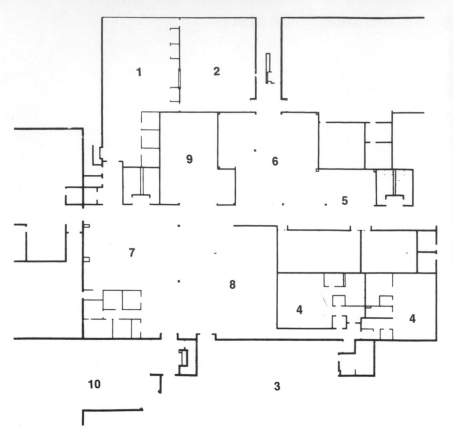

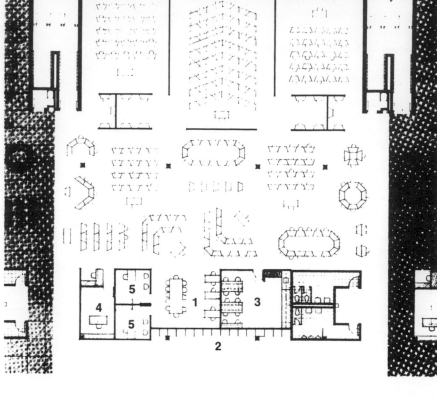

Detail of recreation center:

1 Applied arts
2 Industrial arts
3 Controlled environment facility
4 Recreation locker room
5 Student lockers
6 Dining commons
7 Canteen
8 Game room
9 Club room
10 Recreation entrance

Possible school layout:

1 Seminar
2 Carrels
3 Staff
4 Administration
5 Guidance

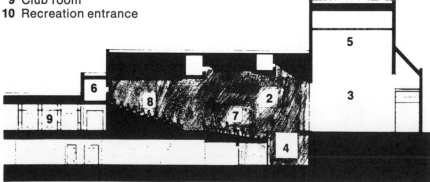

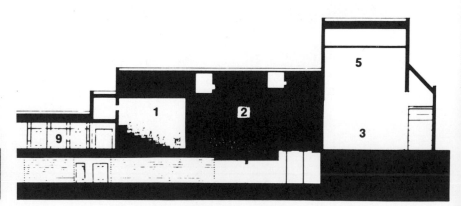

Sections through auditorium:

1 Lecture
2 Auditorium
3 Stage
4 Orchestra pit
5 Fly loft
6 Projection
7 Fixed seating
8 Movable seating
9 Lobby

40 Mini-schools

Owner Mini-school System, Philadelphia, Pennsylvania

Principal Forrest Adams

Architects Merle Lynn Easton, Architectural Design, Philadelphia, Pennsylvania

Occupancy not scheduled

Capacity 120 per block

Organization All grades, K-12

Construction costs $500,000 per typical block

Proposed for Philadelphia but not adopted was this scheme to utilize found space on city blocks to create mini-schools for neighborhood children. The concept requires closing streets, placing portable classroom units in them, and covering the streets with an all-weather plexi-glass dome. The eight-pupil, 240-square-foot units would be equipped with computer terminals and video tubes as well as more conventional materials and equipment. A permanent, octagonal "group experience and teachers' building" would be built into each block.

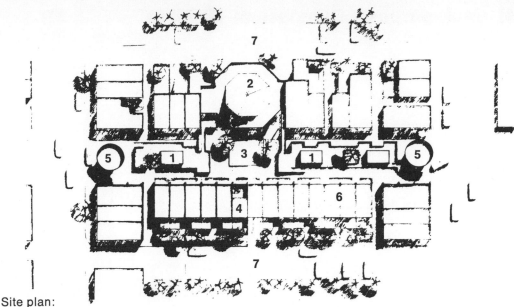

Site plan:

1 Portable student study unit
2 Group experience and teachers' building
3 Amphitheater
4 Private laundry, child care, stores
5 Public toilets
6 Porches
7 Parking and yard improvements

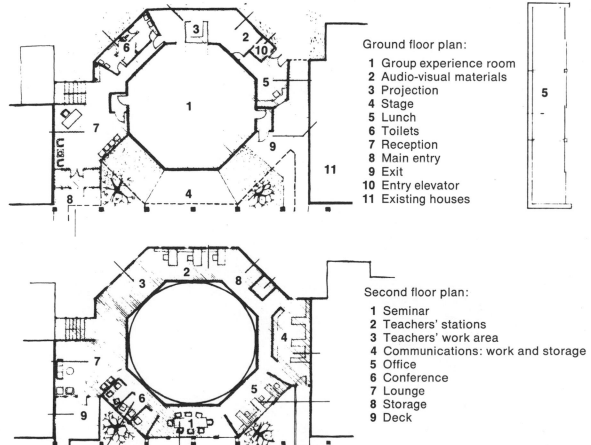

Ground floor plan:

1 Group experience room
2 Audio-visual materials
3 Projection
4 Stage
5 Lunch
6 Toilets
7 Reception
8 Main entry
9 Exit
10 Entry elevator
11 Existing houses

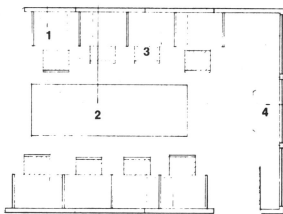

Portable study unit:

1 Study desk
2 Table for group use
3 TV monitors
4 Shelf-projectors
5 Storage closets

Second floor plan:

1 Seminar
2 Teachers' stations
3 Teachers' work area
4 Communications: work and storage
5 Office
6 Conference
7 Lounge
8 Storage
9 Deck

Group experience and teachers' building

41 Multipurpose Gymnasium Building

Owner Normandy School District, Normandy, Missouri

Superintendent Dr. Mel R. Sheehan

Architects William B. Ittner, Inc., St. Louis, Missouri

Project architect Lester C. Haeckel

Engineer Neal J. Campbell

Acoustical consultants Robert Coffeen and Associates

Occupancy September 1968

Capacity 3,040 seats

Organization K-12

Construction costs $1,131,220

This multi-use facility was designed to accommodate not only physical education programs for an adjacent high school but spectator sports, school assemblies, theatrical presentations, and instruction. Retractable backdrops are employed to convert the gymnasium floor into a stage. A partition system, to be added later, will convert one bleacher area into three lecture halls.

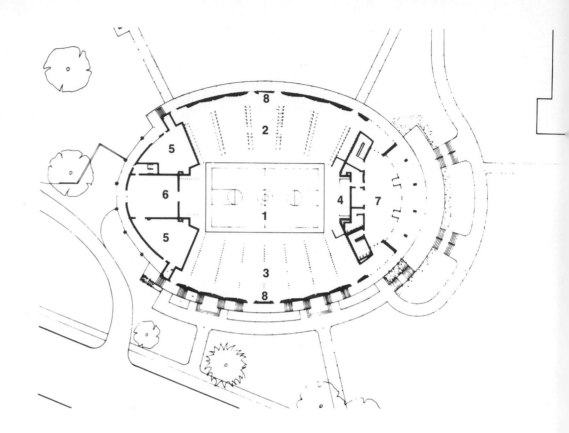

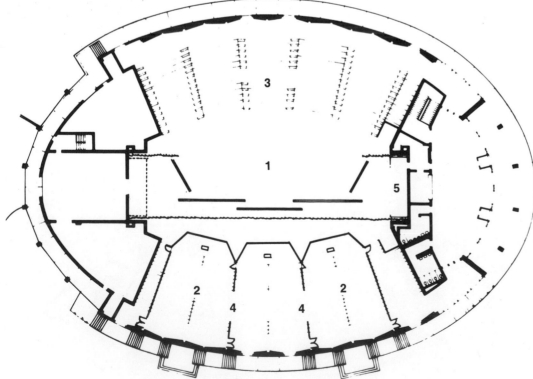

Floor plan:

1 Arena
2 Stadium seats
3 Fixed bleacher seats (locker room underneath)
4 Press box
5 Equipment
6 Service area
7 Lobby
8 Aisle

Use as conventional theater and future lecture hall:

1 Stage
2 Lecture space
3 Stadium seats
4 Movable wall
5 Press box

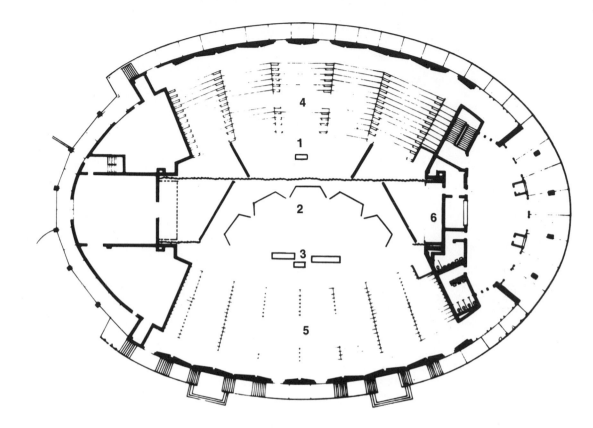

Use as a convention area or for exhibit activities:

1 Lecture space
2 Exhibits
3 Exhibit presentation
4 Stadium seats
5 Fixed bleacher seats
6 Press box

Use as theater in the round:

1 Stage
2 Seating
3 Press box

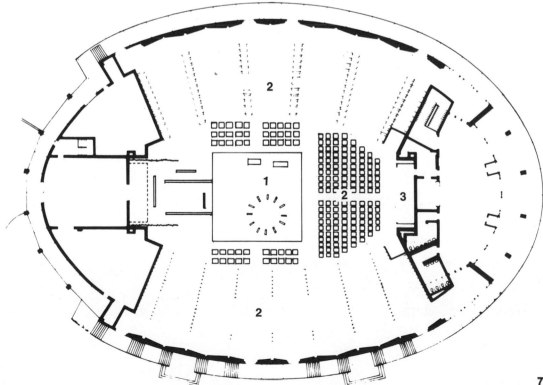

Owner The School District of Philadelphia, Philadelphia, Pennsylvania

Superintendent Dr. Mark Shedd

Associated architects Caudill Rowlett Scott, Houston/New York/Hartford; Bower and Fradley, Philadelphia, Pennsylvania

Occupancy September 1972 (first phase)

Capacity 4,600

Organization 5-12

Construction costs $19,116,000

Originally planned for separate sites, these two urban schools have been combined in a single, shared structure, designed to preserve the identity and autonomy of each. The middle school, to the north, and the high school are separated by a spine including all shared facilities. Within each school, specialized academic areas are on the lower floors, while student houses occupy the top two floors. Open planning prevails throughout the complex to accommodate future educational changes. Shared facilities and outdoor recreation areas are planned for community use.

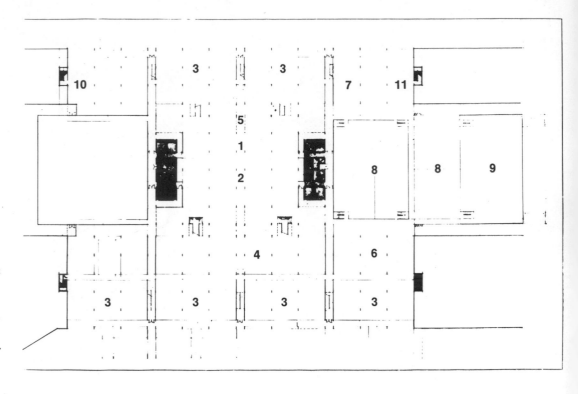

Ground level plan:

1 Middle school art labs
2 High school art labs
3 Shops
4 Home management
5 Music
6 Gymnasium
7 Shop-gymnasium
8 Lockers
9 Pool
10 Kitchen
11 Mechanical

Longitudinal section:

1 Art laboratories
2 Administration
3 Instructional materials center
4 Auditorium
5 Upper auditorium
6 Gymnasium
7 Upper gymnasium
8 Lockers and pool

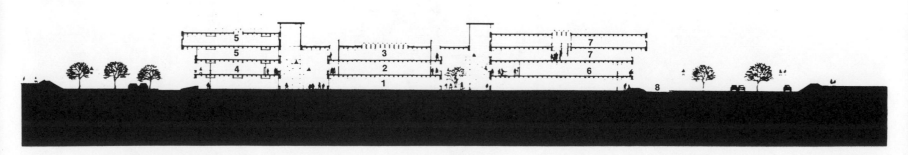

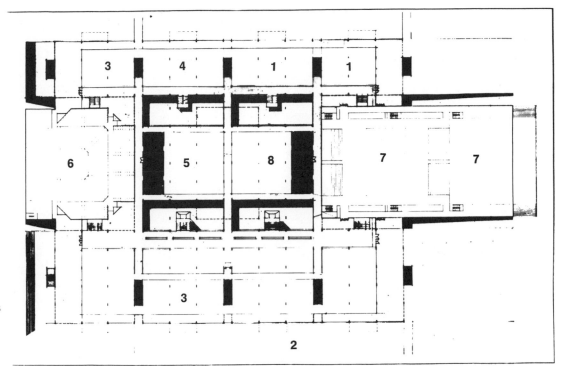

First level plan:

1 Science laboratories
2 Science project laboratories
3 Business laboratories
4 Home management laboratories
5 Administration
6 Auditorium
7 Gymnasium
8 Faculty dining

Second level plan:

1 Middle school house
2 High school house
3 Instructional materials center
4 Upper auditorium
5 Upper gymnasium

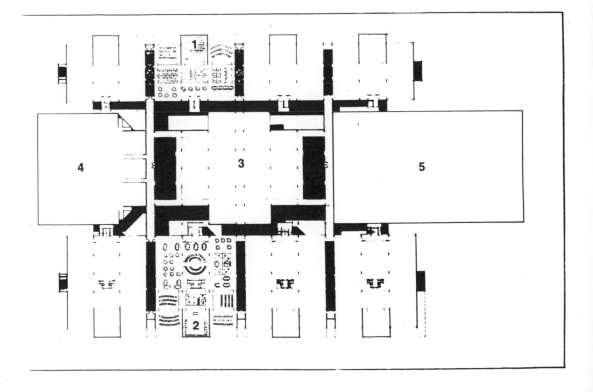

43 LaFollette Middle School/LaFollette Senior High School

Owner Madison Public Schools, Madison, Wisconsin

Superintendent Dr. Douglas Ritchie

High school principal August Vander Meulen

Middle school principal Donald A. Hafeman

Architects John J. Flad & Associates, Madison, Wisconsin

Project architect John P. Reif

Job captain Glenn Johnson

Middle School:

Occupancy January 1969

Capacity 750

Organization 6-8

Project costs $1,400,000

Construction costs $1,200,000

High School:

Occupancy (by phases) September 1964, September 1965, September 1970, January 1971

Capacity 2,800

Organization 9-12

Project costs $6,050,000

Construction costs $5,000,000

These two schools sharing the same site illustrate how changes in a community's educational outlook can be reflected in architecture. While some of the more recent additions to the high school building offer limited flexibility, the essential emphasis on the self-contained classroom of the high school stands in sharp contrast to the relatively open planning of the middle school, which was designed around flexible or modular student scheduling.

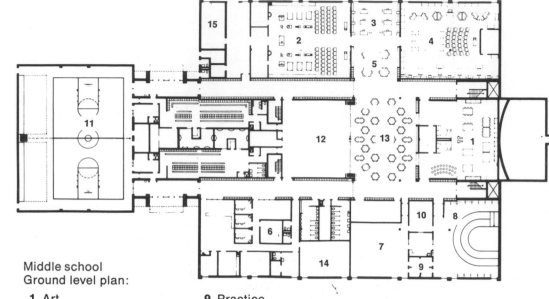

Middle school
Ground level plan:

1	Art	**9**	Practice
2	Industrial arts	**10**	Ensemble
3	Teacher area	**11**	Gymnasium
4	Home economics	**12**	Auxiliary gymnasium
5	Resource area	**13**	Cafeteria - commons
6	Administration and health	**14**	Lounge and dining
7	Choral	**15**	Mechanical
8	Instrumental		

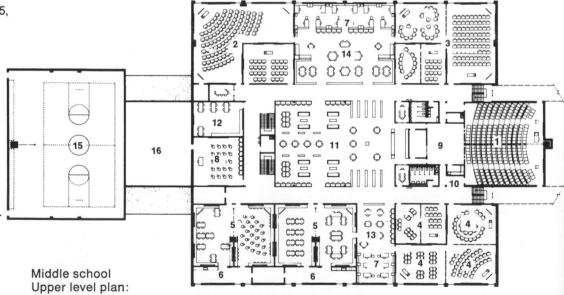

Middle school
Upper level plan:

1	Lecture	**9**	Work and audio-visual area
2	English	**10**	Darkroom
3	Social studies	**11**	Instructional materials center
4	Math	**12**	Reading laboratory
5	Science	**13**	Math - science resource area
6	Preparation	**14**	English - social studies resource area
7	Teacher area	**15**	Gymnasium
8	Language laboratory	**16**	Mechanical equipment room

Site plan:

1 High school
2 Middle school
3 Humanities
4 Business education
5 Laboratories
6 Building trades
7 Gymnasium
8 Gymnasium track

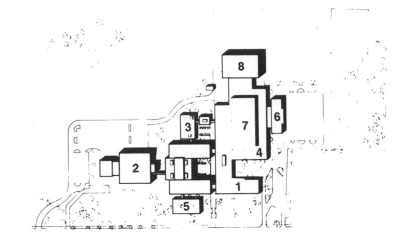

High school
Ground level plan:

1 Classrooms
2 Lecture
3 Business education
4 Art
5 Laboratories
6 Graphic arts
7 Drafting
8 Metals
9 Building trades
10 Automobile mechanics
11 Home economics
12 Humanities resource materials center
13 Science/math resource materials center
14 Administration
15 Guidance
16 Auditorium
17 Band
18 Chorus
19 Gymnasium
20 Gymnasium track
21 Natatorium
22 Cafeteria
23 Faculty dining
24 Commons
25 Mechanical
26 Power mechanical
27 Court

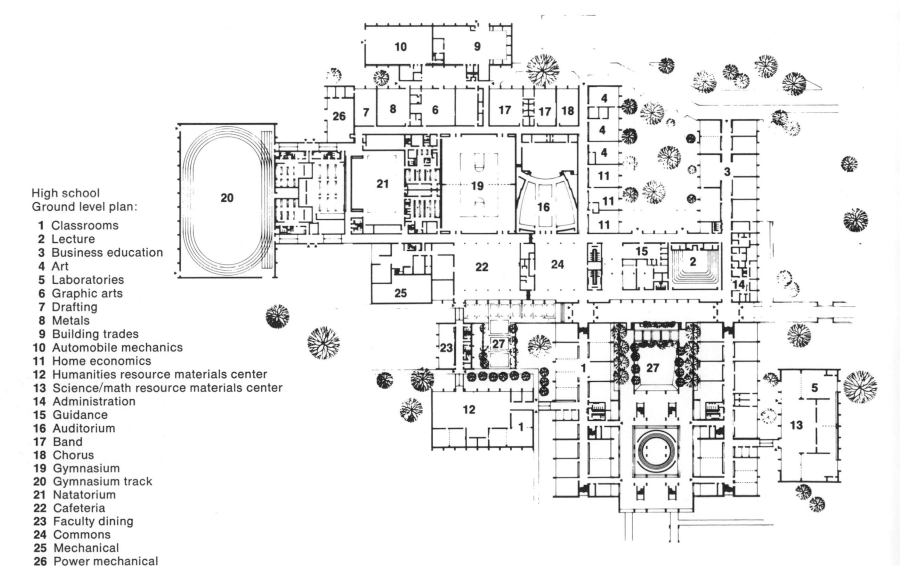

44 Margaret Peck Edwards Hall

Owner Elgin Academy, Elgin, Illinois

Architects Cone & Dornbusch, Chicago, Illinois

Mechanical engineers Mechanical Design, Inc.

Structural engineers Samartano & Associates

Occupancy Fall 1969

Capacity 180

Organization 7-12

Project costs $350,000

Construction costs $281,324

This project offers evidence that educational and architectural change is occurring in private as well as public schools. The building, which replaced a condemned, 100-year-old structure on the campus, houses the Academy's administrative offices, as well as classroom and laboratory space. All fixed partitions are demountable to permit future changes and, in two pairs of classrooms, operable partitions can be opened to accommodate large-group instruction.

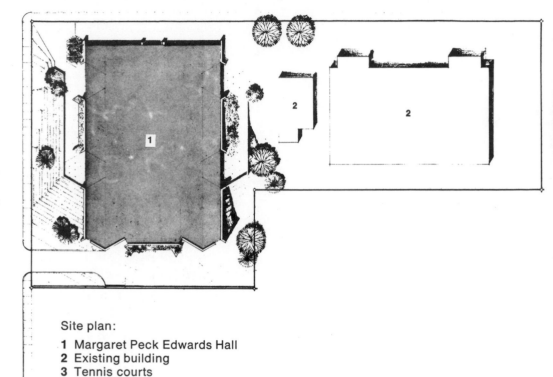

Site plan:

1 Margaret Peck Edwards Hall
2 Existing building
3 Tennis courts
4 Playground
5 Parking area

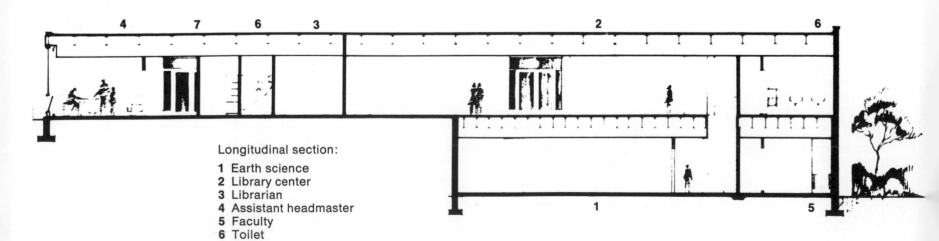

Longitudinal section:

1 Earth science
2 Library center
3 Librarian
4 Assistant headmaster
5 Faculty
6 Toilet
7 Storage

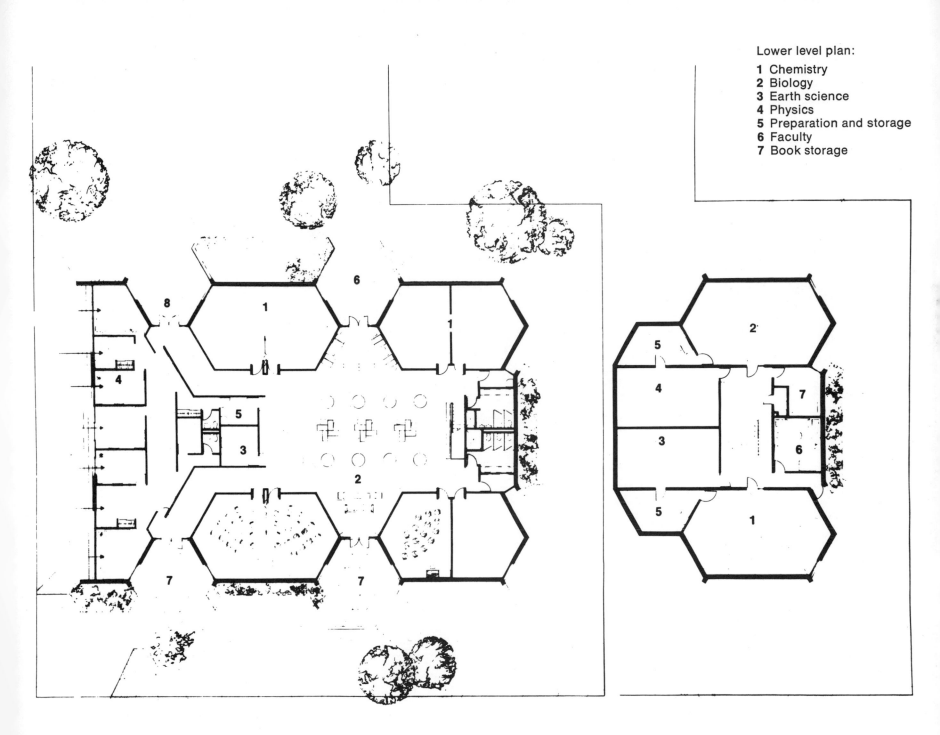

Lower level plan:

1 Chemistry
2 Biology
3 Earth science
4 Physics
5 Preparation and storage
6 Faculty
7 Book storage

Upper level plan:

1 Classroom
2 Library center
3 Librarian
4 Administrative wing
5 Janitor
6 Study terrace
7 Student entrance
8 Public entrance

45 Montgomery Central High School

Owner Montgomery County School System, Clarksville, Tennessee

Director Dr. Max Vann

Principal James Young

Architects Shaver and Company, Salina, Kansas

Project architect Leslie V. Appleby

Mechanical-electrical engineers Burgess, Latimer and Miller

Television and audio-visual Tom Morrissey

Theater consultant James Hull Miller

Furniture and equipment Environmental Planning Associates

Occupancy September 1969

Capacity 1,000

Organization 7-12

Project costs $2,615,935

Construction costs $2,428,451

Evidence that the new education can influence the shape of a schoolhouse, this high school is planned for both immediate and long-term flexibility. The main instructional area on the lower floor is interwoven with instructional materials centers. Teachers' work spaces are located on a balcony overlooking the area. Special instructional spaces — homemaking, science, art, and music — are located in circular building pods overlooking a lake. Teaching spaces range from groups of 300 in the little theater to individual study carrels in the instructional materials areas.

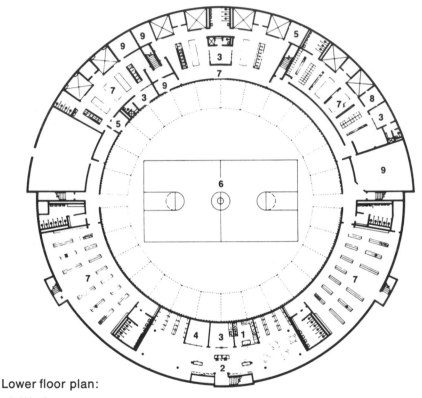

Lower floor plan:

1 Workroom
2 Library
3 Office
4 Conference
5 First aid
6 Gymnasium
7 Lockers
8 Training room
9 Storage

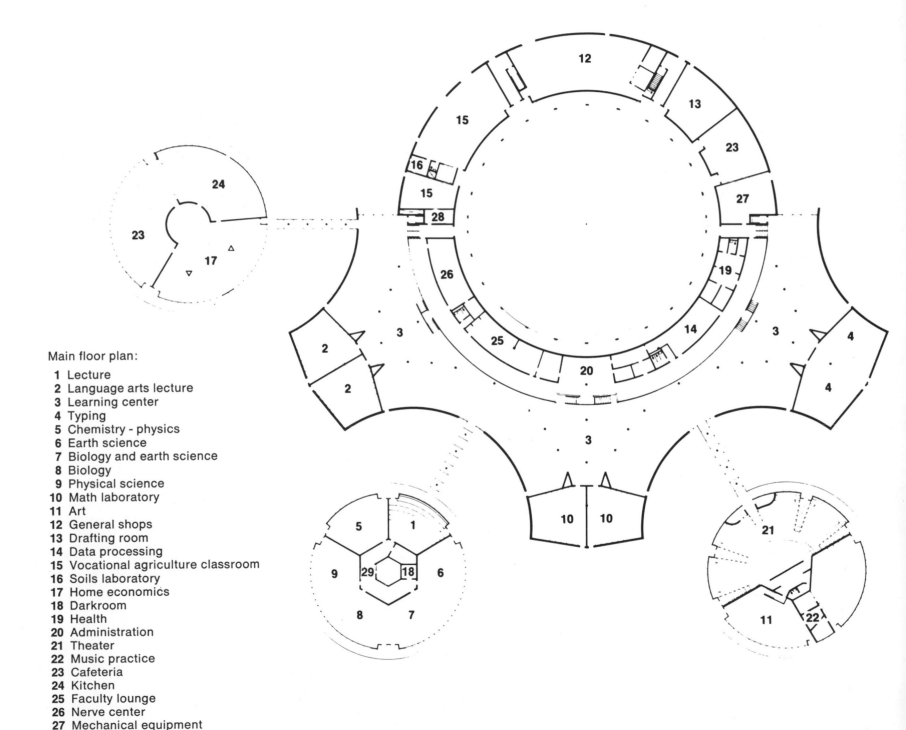

Main floor plan:

1 Lecture
2 Language arts lecture
3 Learning center
4 Typing
5 Chemistry - physics
6 Earth science
7 Biology and earth science
8 Biology
9 Physical science
10 Math laboratory
11 Art
12 General shops
13 Drafting room
14 Data processing
15 Vocational agriculture classroom
16 Soils laboratory
17 Home economics
18 Darkroom
19 Health
20 Administration
21 Theater
22 Music practice
23 Cafeteria
24 Kitchen
25 Faculty lounge
26 Nerve center
27 Mechanical equipment
28 Janitor
29 Storage and preparation

46 Westledge School

Owner Westledge, Inc., Simsbury, Connecticut

Headmaster Louis Feedman

Architects Russell, Gibson & von Dohlen, West Hartford, Connecticut

Project architect John L. Riley

Occupancy 1968 and 1969

Capacity 240

Organization 7-12

Project costs $800,000

Construction costs $670,000

The program for this private day school called for preservation of as much of the rolling, wooded site as possible and for an environment that would encourage contact and the free exchange of ideas between students and faculty. The solution was a campus plan: small-scale buildings housing the different disciplines and physical functions. Of functional interest are the "centrums" or small amphitheaters located in the humanities and science buildings.

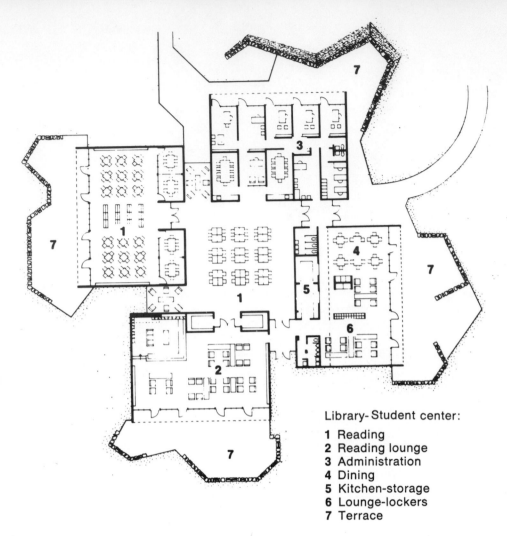

Library- Student center:

1 Reading
2 Reading lounge
3 Administration
4 Dining
5 Kitchen-storage
6 Lounge-lockers
7 Terrace

Humanities center:

1 Classroom
2 Centrum

Science center:

1 Centrum
2 Biology
3 Physics
4 Chemistry
5 Physics projects
6 Biology projects
7 Chemistry projects

Site plan:

1 Humanities center
2 Science laboratory
3 Projects
4 Library-Student center
5 Faculty-Guidance center
6 Dining room
7 Athletic lockers

47 Keota Junior-Senior High School

Owner Keota School District, Keota, Iowa

Superintendent Verdine H. Barnum

Principal Leland Roegner

Architects Hukill-Pfiffner-Alexander-Duenow, Cedar Rapids, Iowa

Occupancy December 1971

Capacity 400

Organization 7-12

Project costs $990,000

Construction costs $761,617

This compact, air-conditioned, carpeted school was designed to provide economical housing for a modern educational program in a small, midwestern community. Of particular interest is the provision of well-defined, enclosed spaces for special functions, and totally open spaces, undefined except by the use of operable partitions, for general instruction. Location of informal classroom space and seminar rooms at the periphery of the library represents an unusual and intriguing solution.

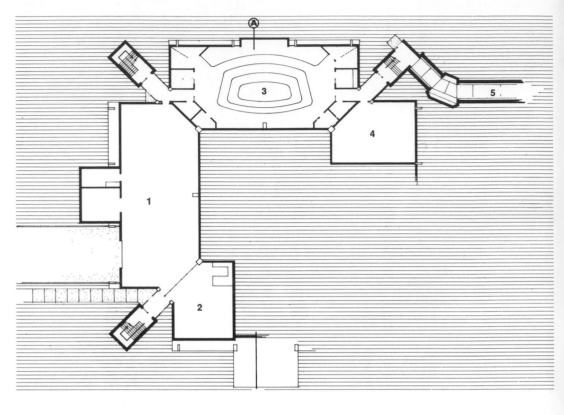

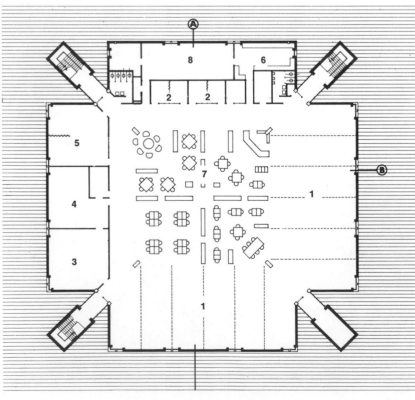

Lower floor plan:

1 Shop
2 Drafting
3 Rehearsal
4 Mechanical
5 Tunnel

Upper floor plan:

1 Classrooms
2 Seminar
3 Typing
4 Bookkeeping
5 Foreign language
6 Workroom
7 Materials center
8 Faculty offices

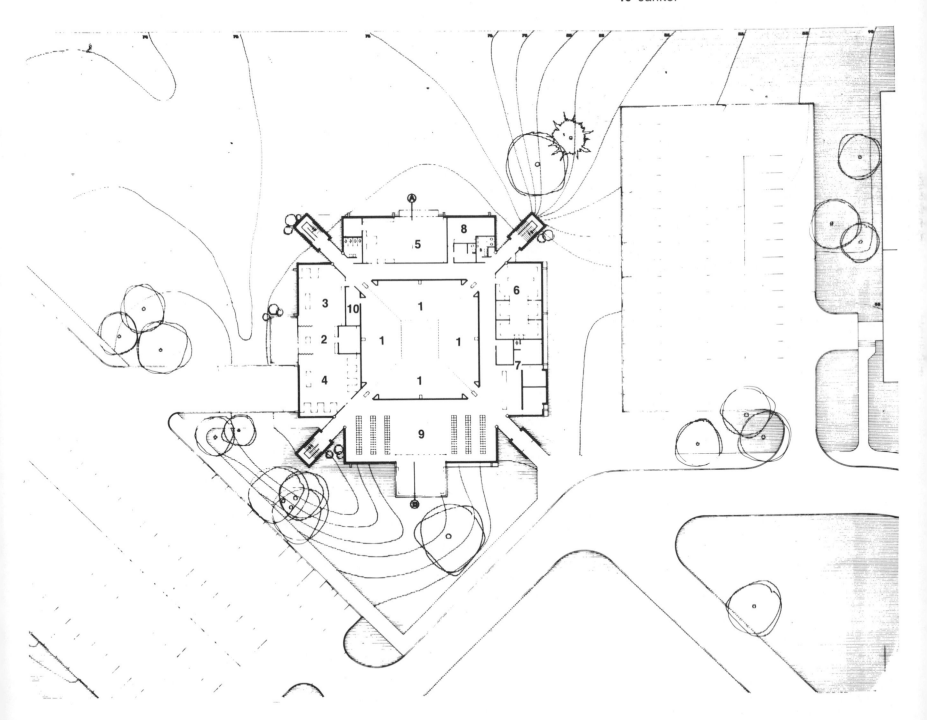

Site plan and Middle floor plan:

1 Classroom
2 Projects
3 Life science
4 Physical science
5 Art
6 Home economics
7 Administration and health
8 Faculty lounge
9 Locker commons
10 Janitor

48 Bartlett/Fort Richardson Junior-Senior High School

Owner Anchorage Borough School District, Anchorage, Alaska

Superintendent Joe D. Montgomery

Associated architects Crittenden Cassetta Wirum & Cannon, San Francisco, California; Hellmuth, Obata & Kassabaum, Inc., St. Louis, Missouri

Project architect Ed Crittenden

Occupancy January 1973

Capacity 3,000

Organization 7-12

Project costs $14,000,000

Construction costs $11,400,000

This combined junior-senior high school is designed around a modern program calling for flexible instructional groupings and long-term structural flexibility. A loft plan provides 60-foot clear spans, within which space can be arranged and rearranged as required. The lofts are kept clear by removing restrooms, stairs, mechanical equipment, and other fixed elements to towerlike structures at their periphery. The two schools share common facilities — library, theater, music rooms, physical education facilities, and industrial arts laboratories — all located at the center of the complex.

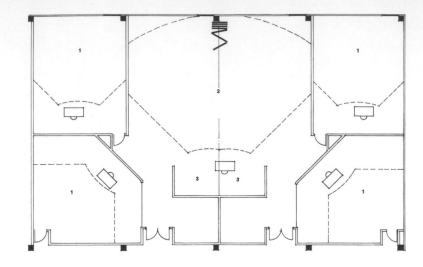

Typical classroom cluster:

1 30-seat units
2 Divisible classroom — 60-seat unit
3 Seminar

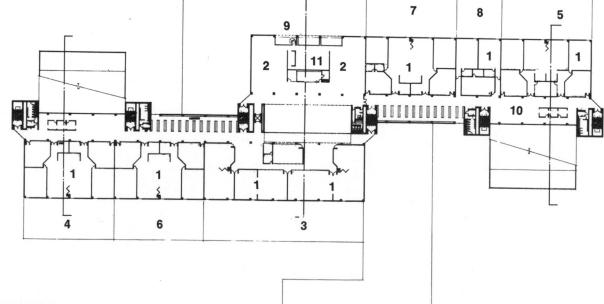

Upper level floor plan:

1 Classroom cluster
2 Teachers' work stations
3 Business
4 Junior high math
5 Senior high math
6 Junior high language
7 Senior high language
8 Language laboratory
9 Open to instructional materials center below
10 Student activities center
11 Faculty lounge

49 Upper School

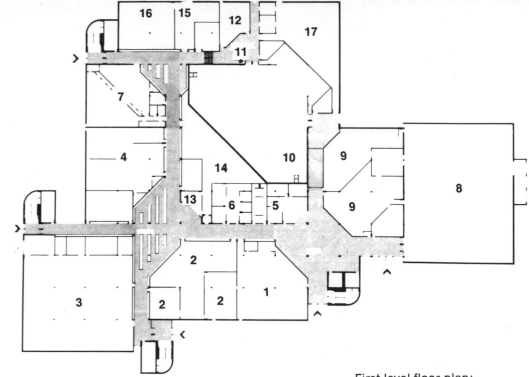

Owner Maine School Administrative District No. 75, Maine

Superintendent Ralph Ulmer

Architects Drummey Rosane Anderson, Inc., Newton Lower Falls, Massachusetts

In charge David W. Anderson

Project manager Robert Miller

Project designer William Nemmers

Occupancy September 1972

Capacity 1,300

Organization 7-12

Project costs $4,480,000

Construction costs $3,700,000

This combined junior-senior high school, which will serve a number of small Maine communities, boasts a combination of standard classrooms and large open teaching spaces to provide flexibility and easy adaptation to changing curriculum and new educational techniques. Teaching areas open into an educational resource center, which in turn is linked to a commons. The commons, serving as dining area and auditorium, also provides overflow space for the library and for special projects.

First level floor plan:

1 Art
2 Business education
3 Shops
4 Home economics
5 Health and administration
6 Guidance
7 Music
8 Gymnasium
9 Lockers
10 Commons
11 Serving
12 Kitchen
13 Teachers' room
14 Bookstore
15 Storage
16 Custodial
17 Boiler

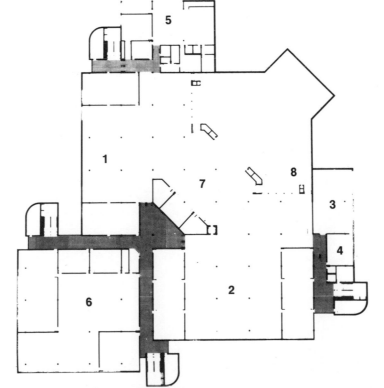

Second level floor plan:

1 7-8 grade classrooms
2 9-12 grade classrooms
3 Special education
4 Remedial
5 Teacher workrooms
6 Science suite
7 Library
8 Commons

50 North Kingstown High School Addition

Owner North Kingstown School Department, North Kingstown, Rhode Island

Superintendent Dr. Lawrence A. McGuire

Principal George T. Sprague

Architects The Providence Partnership, Providence, Rhode Island

Educational consultant Dr. Sidney P. Rollins

Special equipment design Research & Design Institute

Occupancy September 1970

Capacity 1,000 (first phase), 2,000 (total)

Organization 9-12

Construction costs $2,179,000

The "great room," a vast open expanse, 150 by 210 feet, 31,500 square feet, is the instructional focal point of this new high school addition. The room is furnished with specially designed, free-standing or rolling furniture and equipment, which permits maximum flexibility in teaching arrangements and provides visual privacy where required. Acoustic privacy is obtained through the use of carpeting and acoustical ceilings and utilization of the public address system to introduce masking noise into the room. A divisible auditorium-lecture hall is provided for large-group instruction.

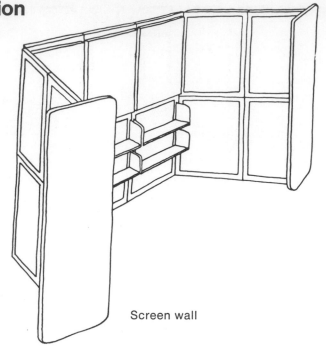

Screen wall

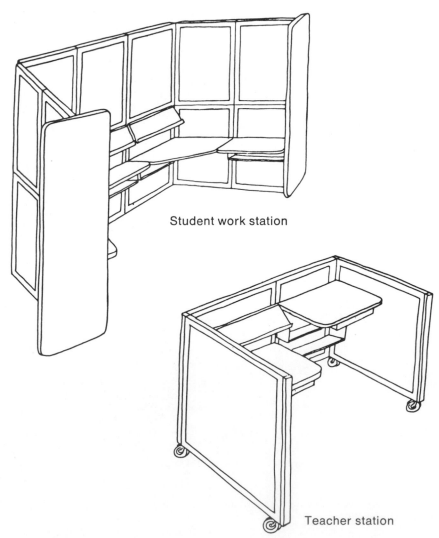

Student work station

Teacher station

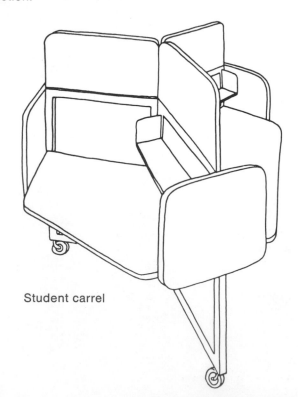

Student carrel

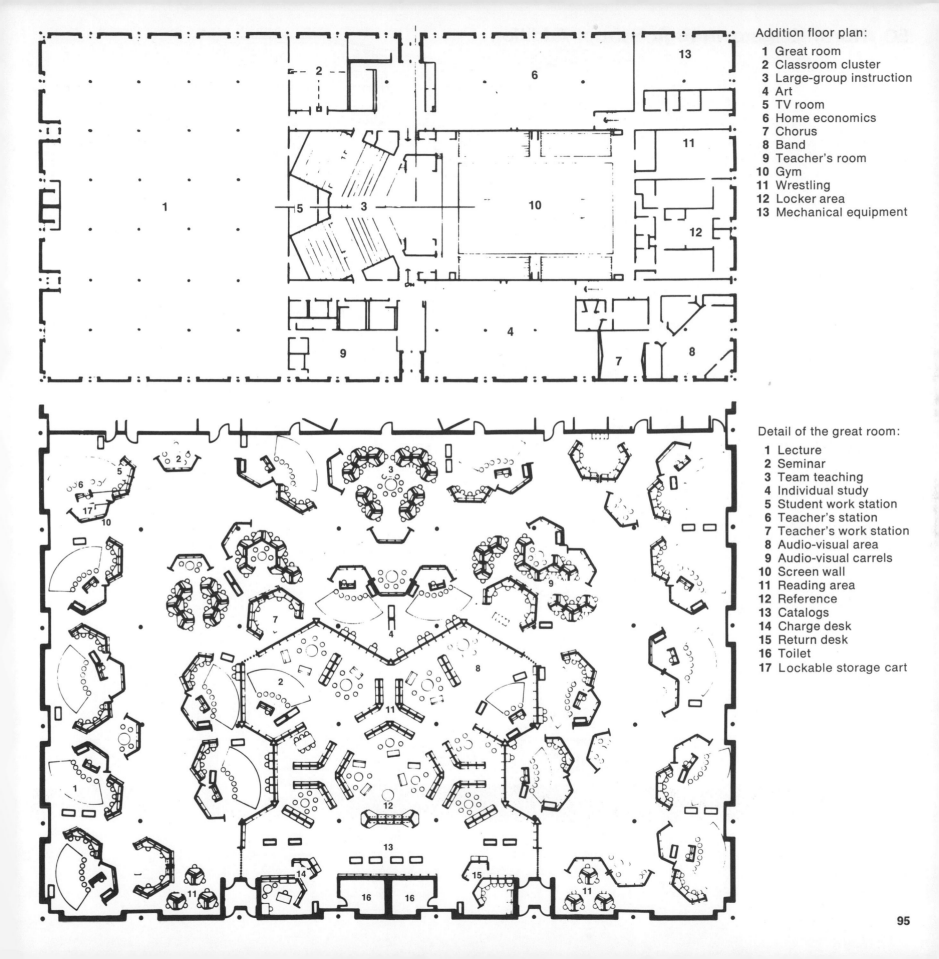

Addition floor plan:

1 Great room
2 Classroom cluster
3 Large-group instruction
4 Art
5 TV room
6 Home economics
7 Chorus
8 Band
9 Teacher's room
10 Gym
11 Wrestling
12 Locker area
13 Mechanical equipment

Detail of the great room:

1 Lecture
2 Seminar
3 Team teaching
4 Individual study
5 Student work station
6 Teacher's station
7 Teacher's work station
8 Audio-visual area
9 Audio-visual carrels
10 Screen wall
11 Reading area
12 Reference
13 Catalogs
14 Charge desk
15 Return desk
16 Toilet
17 Lockable storage cart

51 A New Queens High School

Owner New York City Board of Education, New York, New York

Chancellor Dr. Harvey B. Scribner

Architects Welton Becket and Associates, Los Angeles, California

Project architect Arthur Knapp

Structural engineer Wayman King

Mechanical-electrical engineer Joseph R. Loring

Site and landscaping McFarland-Johnson-Gibbons

Occupancy Fall 1972

Capacity 4,000

Organization 9-12

Project costs $18,550,000

Construction costs $15,860,000

The self-contained classroom remains very much in evidence in this plan for a New York City high school. However, the strong departmental organization of the school layout includes provision for a large, open room, or "flexible group complex," for each department. These provide an opportunity for flexibility in instructional groupings. Both the auditorium and cafeteria are divisible, providing additional instructional spaces of varying sizes.

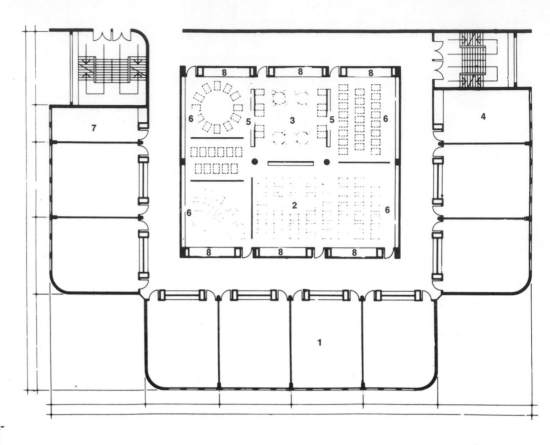

Typical classroom cluster:

1 Typical classroom
2 Flexible group complex
3 Resource center
4 Department office
5 Movable bookshelves
6 Student lockers
7 Teachers' rest room
8 Storage

Longitudinal section:

1 Classroom
2 Library
3 Reading room
4 Health
5 Health education
6 Auditorium
7 Auditorium stage
8 Gymnasium
9 Locker room
10 Cafeteria
11 Mechanical

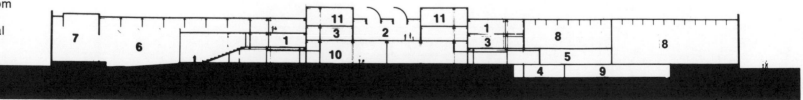

First floor plan:

1 Classroom
2 Special education
3 Speech department
4 Shop wing
5 Administration, conference, and
   guidance wing
6 Auditorium
7 Music area
8 Gymnasium wing
9 Dining
10 Kitchen
11 Mechanical wing
12 Shop court
13 Service court

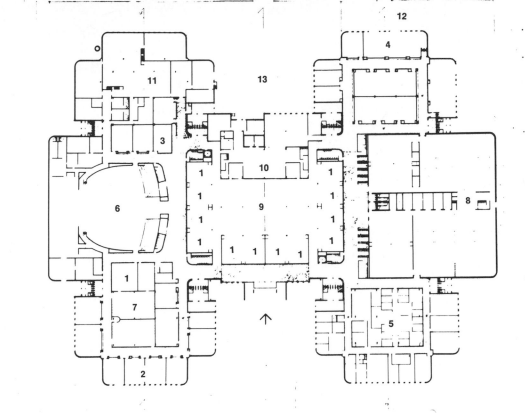

Third floor plan:

1 Social studies classrooms
2 Social studies flexible group complex
3 Foreign language classrooms
4 Foreign language flexible group complex
5 Science classroom wing
6 Science laboratories
7 Language laboratories
8 Art classrooms
9 Art studio
10 Shop wing
11 3-unit shop
12 Open to library below
13 Upper part of auditorium
14 Upper part of gymnasium
15 Mechanical
16 Upper part of mechanical equipment

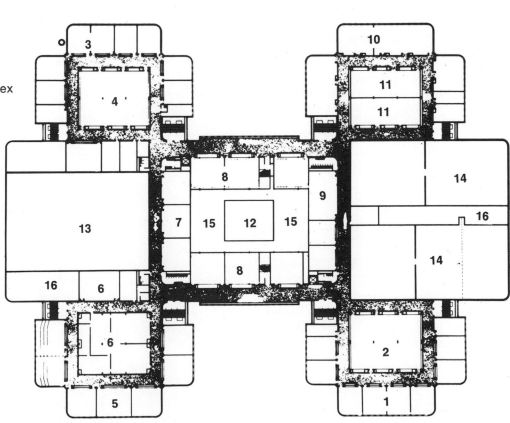

52 Wilton Senior High School

Owner Town of Wilton, Connecticut

Superintendent Dr. Clayton L. Akin

Principal Joseph Brence

Associated architects Robert H. Schofield, Nyack, New York; Earl R. Flansburgh, Cambridge, Massachusetts

Educational consultant Dr. Cyril G. Sargent

Structural engineer Zorab Vosganian

Mechanical-electrical engineers Kallen & Lemelson

Acoustics Bolt, Beranek & Newman, Inc.

Occupancy September 1971

Capacity 2,000 (first phase), 2,500 (future expansion)

Organization 9-12

Project costs $12,000,000

Construction costs $9,500,000

Planned for an educational program stressing individualized instruction and for community use, this high school emerged as a series of resource areas: an instructional materials center, a laboratory area, a general instructional area, and a field house for physical education and related activities. The instructional materials center and field house both are in separate structures, connected by bridges to the main building, which facilitates community use without disrupting school operations. General classroom areas are arranged so that they can be combined or subdivided to provide spaces ranging from seminar to large-group instruction areas.

Cross section:
1 Classroom
2 Home economics
3 Main reading level
4 Upper reading level
5 Student area
6 Mechanical
7 Boiler room
8 Entry

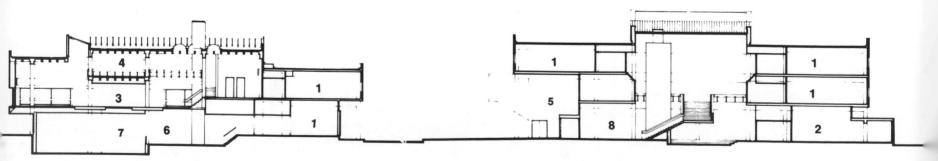

First floor plan:

1 Classrooms
2 Lecture hall
3 Science
4 Laboratories
5 Fine arts
6 Industrial arts
7 Home economics
8 Audio-visual area
9 Theater
10 Band
11 Choral
12 Field house
13 Auxiliary gymnasium
14 Student offices and social area
15 Mechanical room
16 Greenhouse

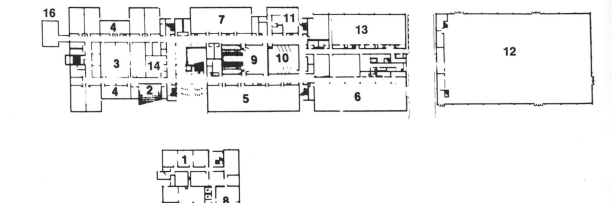

Second floor plan:

1 Classrooms
2 Lecture hall
3 Seminars
4 Business - mathematics
5 Resource center - lower reading room
6 Administration, health, guidance
7 Theater upper level
8 Field house
9 Lockers
10 Cafeteria - commons
11 Faculty dining

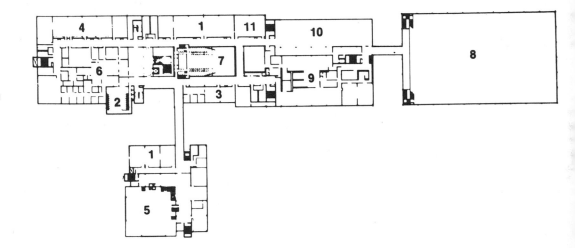

Third floor plan:

1 English classrooms
2 Social studies classrooms
3 Language classrooms
4 Language laboratories
5 Future classrooms
6 Teacher workrooms
7 Upper reading area
8 Field house
9 Open court

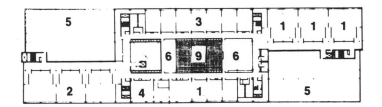
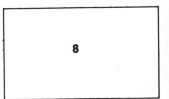
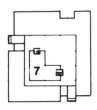

53 West Bend High School

Owner West Bend Board of Education, West Bend, Wisconsin

Superintendent John D. Bowser

Superintendent during planning Donald H. Peckenpaugh

Architects Welton Becket and Associates, Chicago, Illinois

Occupancy 1970

Capacity 2,500 (first phase), 5,000 (ultimate)

Organization 9-12

Construction costs $6,072,258

The emphasis here is on the house plan or school-within-a-school concept. Each school of 1,250 pupils is a self-sufficient unit, with its own offices, cafeteria, library, and the full range of instructional spaces, including lecture halls. Standard classrooms are divisible into seminar spaces. A divisible auditorium provides additional large-group teaching space.

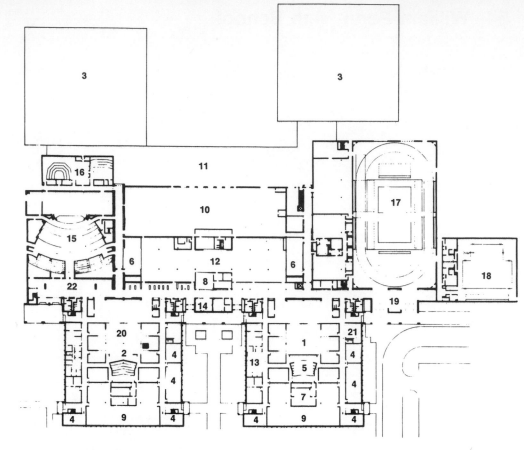

First floor plan:

1 Academic School A
2 Academic School B
3 Future academic school
4 Classroom
5 Group instruction
6 Large group room
7 Staff preparation
8 Studio
9 Science education area
10 Prevocational shop area
11 Future prevocational expansion
12 Visual communication area
13 Administration
14 Health
15 Auditorium
16 Music
17 Main gymnasium and fieldhouse
18 Natatorium
19 Ticket office
20 Cafeteria - group instruction
21 Faculty room
22 Lobby

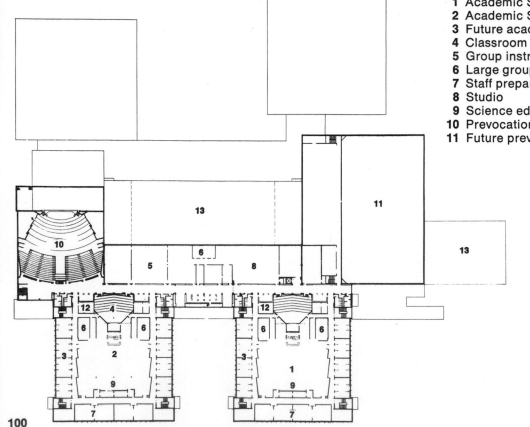

Second floor plan:

1 Academic School A
2 Academic School B
3 Classrooms
4 Large group room
5 Business subjects
6 Staff preparation
7 Language laboratory
8 Home economics
9 Library resource center
10 Upper auditorium
11 Upper gymnasium
12 Student publications
13 Roof

54 William Penn High School

Owner The School District of Philadelphia, Philadelphia, Pennsylvania

Superintendent Dr. Mark R. Shedd

Principal Mrs. Odette Harris

Architects Mitchell/Giurgola Associates, Philadelphia, Pennsylvania

Project architects William Fox, Joel Baillere

Structural engineers Keast & Hood

Mechanical engineers Vinokur/Pace

Electrical engineer Donald Nardy

Acoustics Robert Hansen

Occupancy June 1973

Capacity 3,000 (first phase), 4,000 (ultimate)

Organization 9-12

Construction costs $19,000,000

An interesting approach to the clustering of classroom space marks this architecturally intriguing plan for a new urban high school. A "magnet" school, the new facility will specialize in communications — journalism, radio, TV, theater — and draw students majoring in these subjects from neighborhoods throughout the city. It is designed for eventual expansion to an enrollment of 4,000 and for extensive community use. Academically, it is divided into six identical houses of 500 students each.

Site plan:
1 Fine arts
2 Instructional materials center
3 Administration
4 Child development
5 Gymnasium
6 Pool
7 Dining
8 Sitting area
9 Court games
10 Playing field
11 Play area
12 Houses

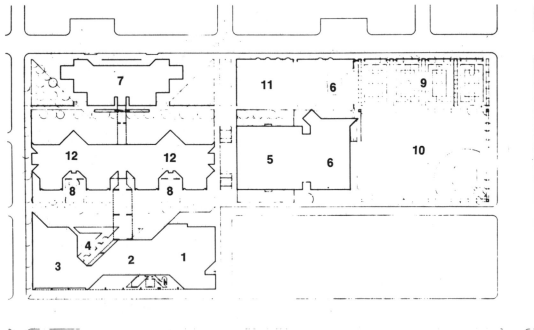

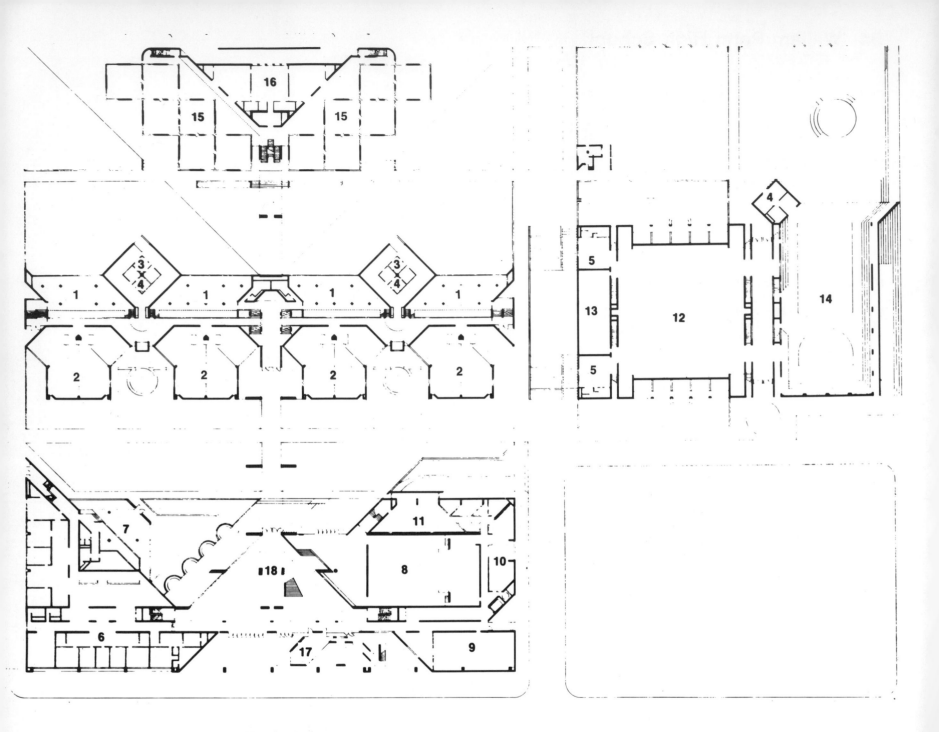

First level plan:

1 Learning center
2 House classroom unit
3 Classrooms above
4 Faculty offices
5 Instructors' office
6 Administration
7 Child development
8 Theater
9 Experimental theater
10 Stage craft
11 Music
12 Gymnasium
13 Remedial reading
14 Pool
15 Student dining
16 Kitchen
17 Book store
18 Entrance court

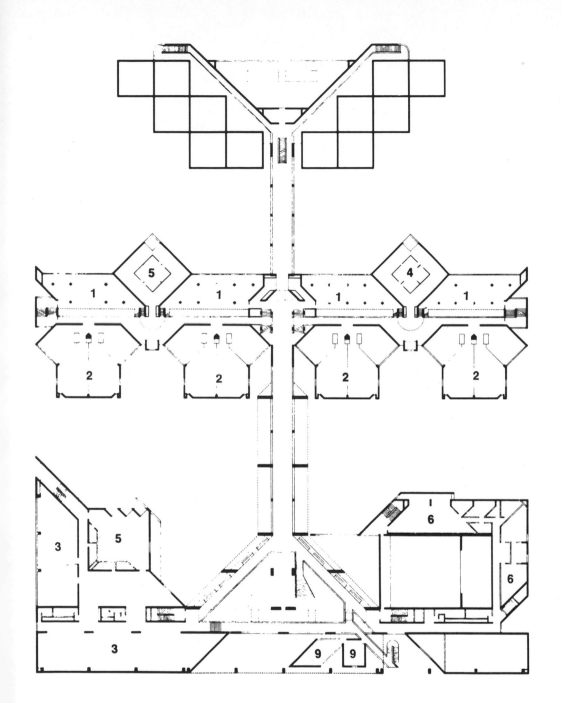
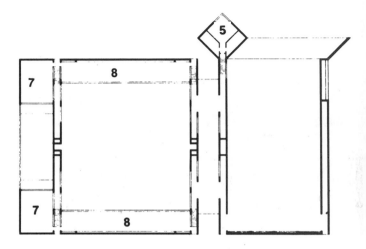

Second level plan:

1 Learning center
2 House classroom unit
3 Home arts classroom
4 Classrooms above
5 Faculty offices
6 Music
7 Gymnasium station
8 Bleachers
9 Student activity offices

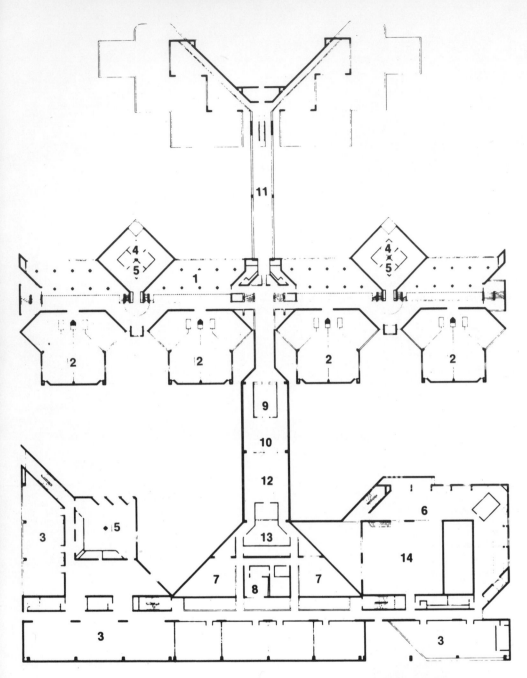

Third level plan:

1 Learning center
2 House classroom unit
3 Commerce classroom
4 Classrooms above
5 Faculty offices
6 Art studios
7 TV studio
8 Radio studio
9 Library above
10 Electronic carrels
11 Faculty dining
12 Staff area
13 Central control
14 Roof terrace

55 Herbert H. Lehman High School

Owner New York City Board of Education, New York, New York

Superintendent Dr. Harvey B. Scribner

Architects The Eggers Partnership (formerly Eggers and Higgins) New York, New York

Project architect John B. Hayden

Structural engineers Purdy and Henderson

Mechanical engineers Ebner-Schmidt Associates

Occupancy May 1972

Capacity 4,000

Organization 9-12

Construction costs $19,500,000

This otherwise-conventional urban high school boasts one unique and highly significant feature: its use of air rights over the Hutchinson River Parkway in the Bronx. A three-story bridge over the parkway connects the main academic building with the auditorium-music facilities. The air-rights solution was prompted by the fact that the site consisted of two parcels, one on either side of the parkway and neither adequate to accommodate the entire school. Such an air-rights solution to schoolhouse architecture may have interesting implications for urban school systems faced with the problem of condemning tax-producing real estate and relocating residents to provide school sites.

Site plan:
1 Classrooms
2 Administration
3 Auditorium
4 Music
5 Gymnasium
6 Athletic field
7 Westchester Creek

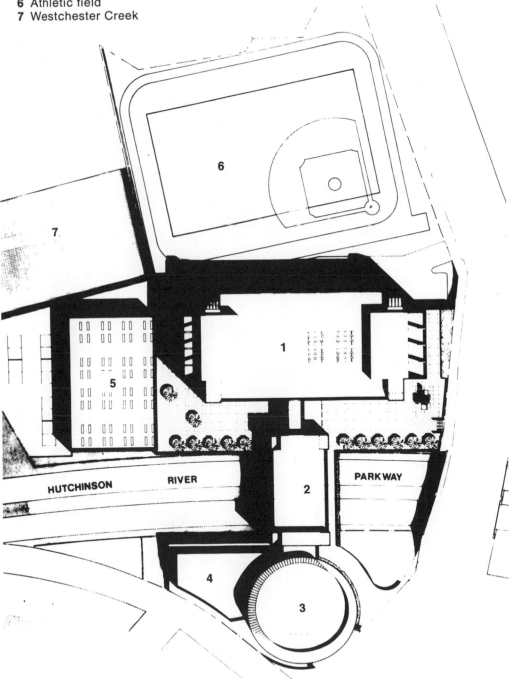

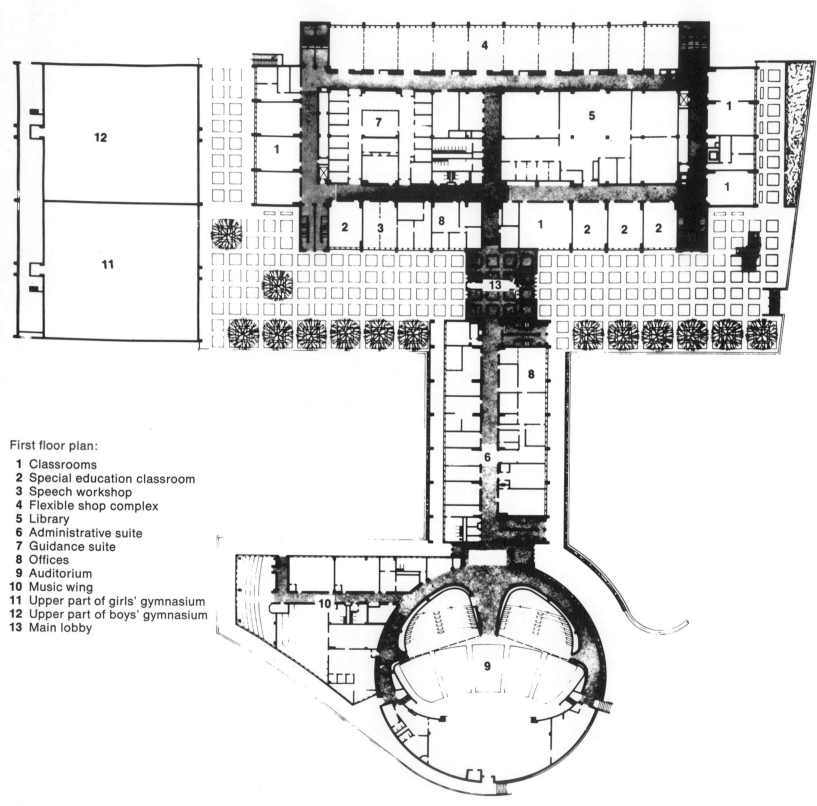

First floor plan:

1 Classrooms
2 Special education classroom
3 Speech workshop
4 Flexible shop complex
5 Library
6 Administrative suite
7 Guidance suite
8 Offices
9 Auditorium
10 Music wing
11 Upper part of girls' gymnasium
12 Upper part of boys' gymnasium
13 Main lobby

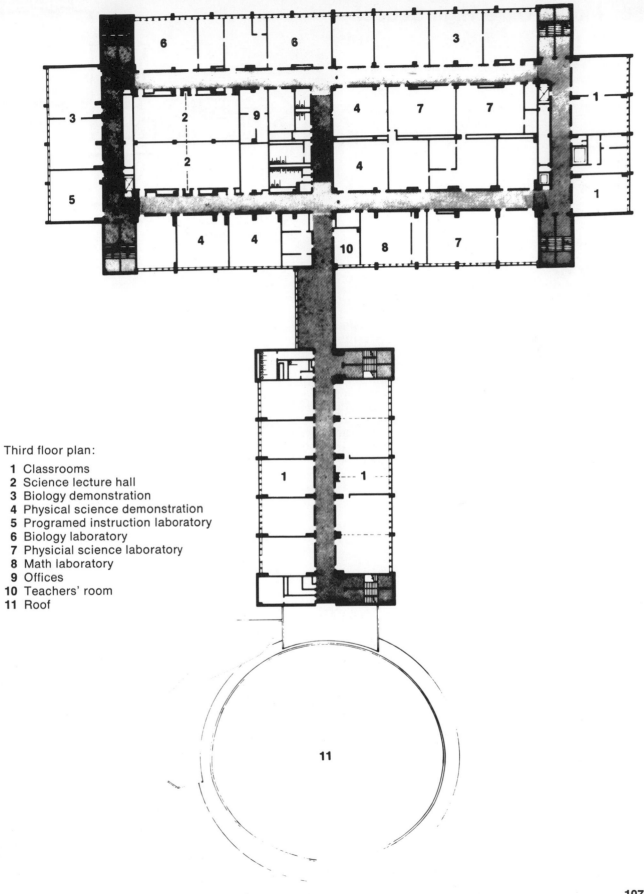

Third floor plan:

1 Classrooms
2 Science lecture hall
3 Biology demonstration
4 Physical science demonstration
5 Programed instruction laboratory
6 Biology laboratory
7 Physicial science laboratory
8 Math laboratory
9 Offices
10 Teachers' room
11 Roof

56 Mount Olive High School

Owner West Morris Regional High School District, Chester, New Jersey

Superintendent Dr. Robert W. Young

Architects Uniplan, Princeton, New Jersey

Principal-in-charge Jules Gregory

Occupancy Fall 1972

Capacity 1,000

Organization 9-12

Project costs $4,000,000

Construction costs $3,000,000

A double-decker, divisible auditorium is the outstanding feature of this high school plan. The 600 seats, arranged in two tiers on three sides of the open, central stage, can be partitioned off to create six large-group instructional areas, each seating 100. It is estimated that the auditorium will be in use 85 per cent of the school week, rather than the 15 per cent utilization normally found in conventional auditoriums. Other instructional spaces are planned around the school's conventional classrooms but, because all interior partitions are demountable, the spaces are also adaptable to future changes in instructional patterns.

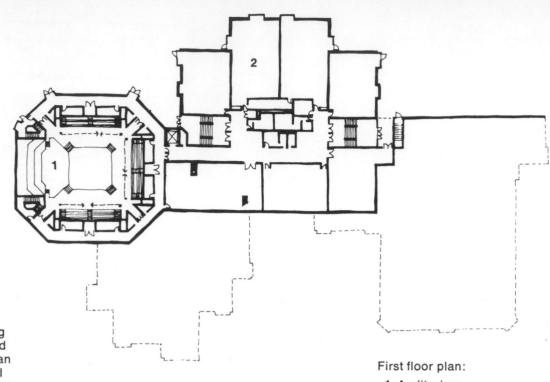

First floor plan:
1 Auditorium
2 Related arts

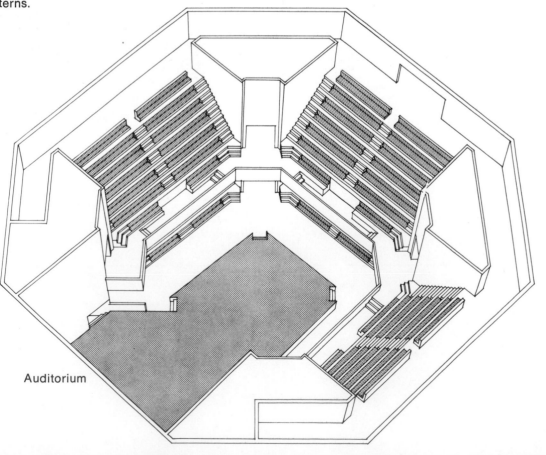

Auditorium

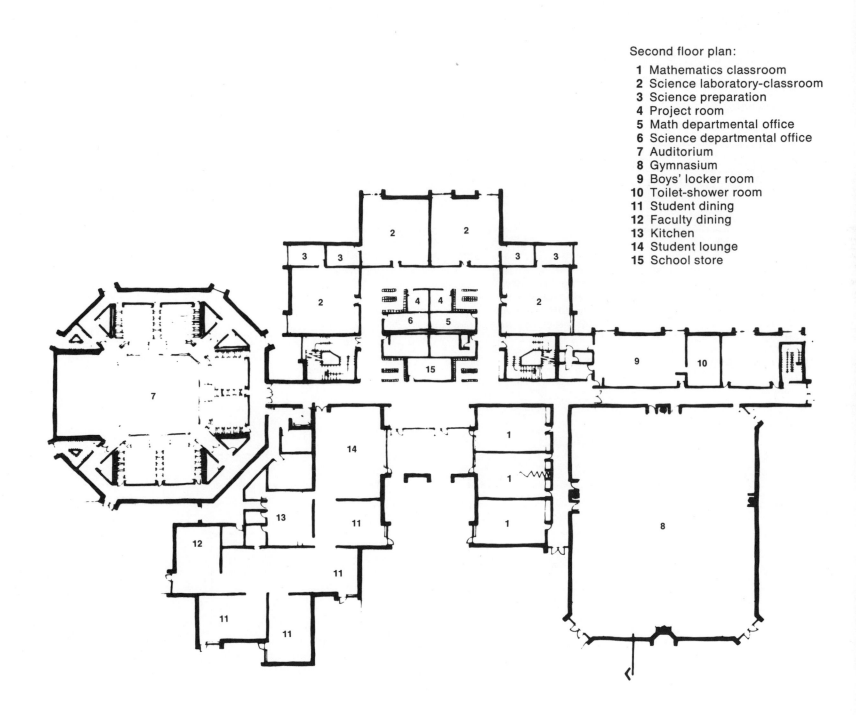

Second floor plan:

1 Mathematics classroom
2 Science laboratory-classroom
3 Science preparation
4 Project room
5 Math departmental office
6 Science departmental office
7 Auditorium
8 Gymnasium
9 Boys' locker room
10 Toilet-shower room
11 Student dining
12 Faculty dining
13 Kitchen
14 Student lounge
15 School store

57 Lincoln West High School

Owner City of Cleveland Public Schools, Cleveland, Ohio

Superintendent Dr. Paul W. Briggs

Architects Ward Associates Architects, Cleveland, Ohio

Structural engineers Barber & Hoffman

Mechanical engineers Pfitzenmaier & Jablonski

Electrical engineers Paul C. Mehnert & Associates

Occupancy September 1970

Capacity 3,000

Organization 10-12

Project costs $6,500,000

Construction costs $6,000,000

A tight, urban site and the decision to air condition prompted this compact plan for a high school. To offset the anonymity of a large school population, each of the three grades is housed on its own floor for all activities except industrial arts, fine arts, home economics, music, and physical education. An unusual feature is an indoor running track at the balcony-level perimeter of the gymnasium and auditorium.

First floor plan:
1 Classrooms
2 Biology
3 Advanced science
4 Seminars
5 Typing
6 Arts
7 Shops
8 Clothing
9 Foods
10 Service station training area
11 Administration
12 Planning room
13 Music
14 Library
15 Reading - lunch
16 Kitchen

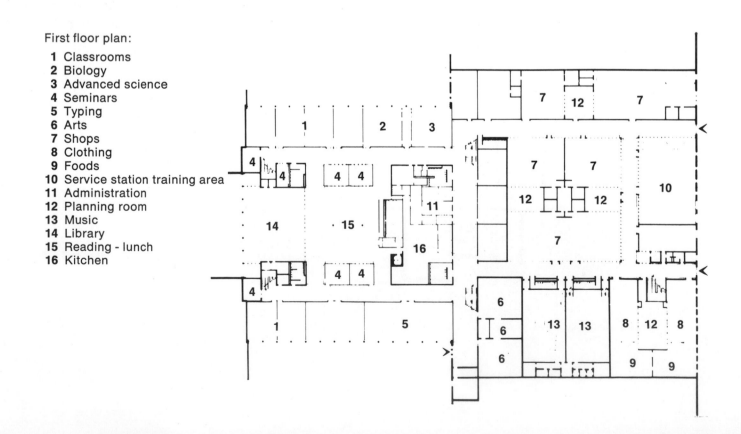

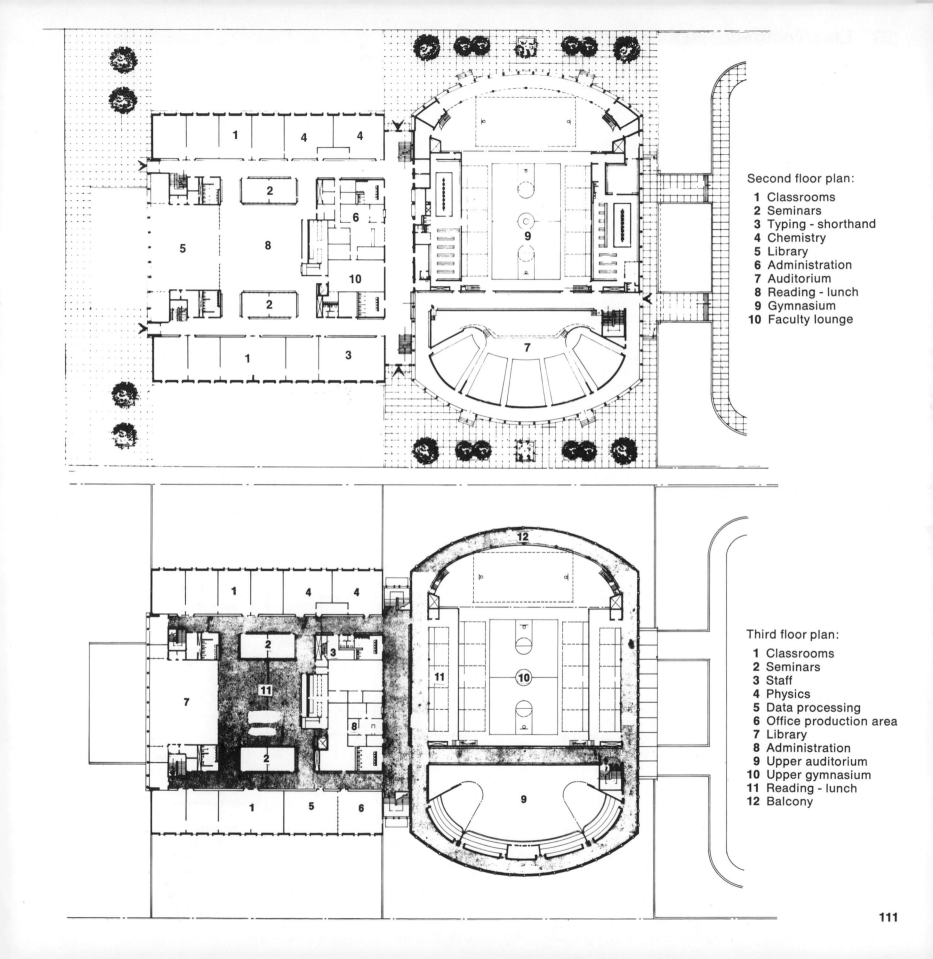

Second floor plan:

1 Classrooms
2 Seminars
3 Typing - shorthand
4 Chemistry
5 Library
6 Administration
7 Auditorium
8 Reading - lunch
9 Gymnasium
10 Faculty lounge

Third floor plan:

1 Classrooms
2 Seminars
3 Staff
4 Physics
5 Data processing
6 Office production area
7 Library
8 Administration
9 Upper auditorium
10 Upper gymnasium
11 Reading - lunch
12 Balcony

58 East Technical High School

Owner City of Cleveland Public Schools, Cleveland, Ohio

Superintendent Dr. Paul Briggs

Architects Dela Motte, Larson, Nassau & Associates, Cleveland, Ohio

Occupancy September 1973

Capacity 2,000

Organization 10-12

Construction costs $9,614,080

Planned as a replacement for an existing and prestigious Cleveland institution, this design calls for a school-within-a-school approach, providing intimacy and a sense of identity in a 2,000-pupil school. Each grade is assigned to its own floor. With the exception of auditorium, physical education, shop, and other highly specialized facilities, each floor, or "school," is self-sufficient and complete with its own library, cafeteria and instructional facilities.

Longitudinal section:
1 Classroom
2 Math
3 Physics
4 Chemistry
5 Language laboratory
6 Sophomore library
7 Junior library
8 Senior library
9 Administration
10 Gymnasium
11 Pool
12 Running track
13 Team room
14 Lockers
15 Court

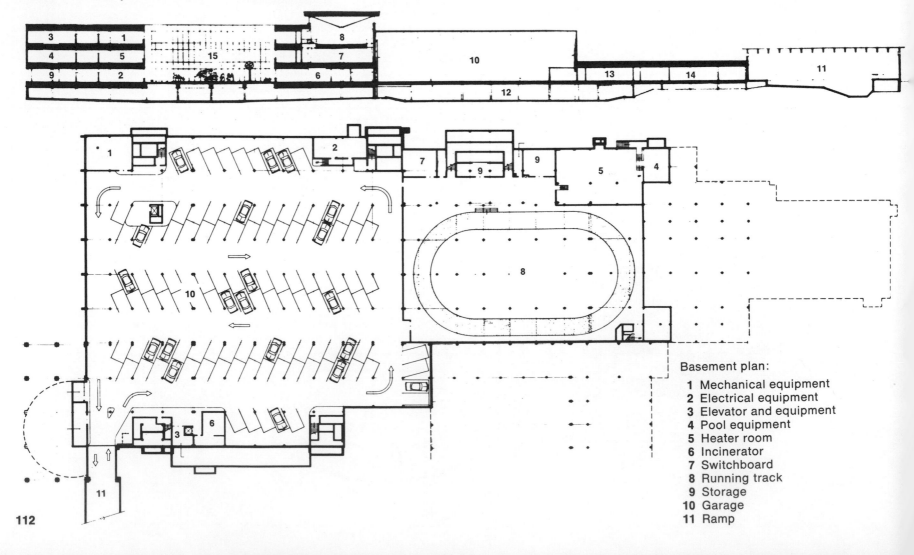

Basement plan:
1 Mechanical equipment
2 Electrical equipment
3 Elevator and equipment
4 Pool equipment
5 Heater room
6 Incinerator
7 Switchboard
8 Running track
9 Storage
10 Garage
11 Ramp

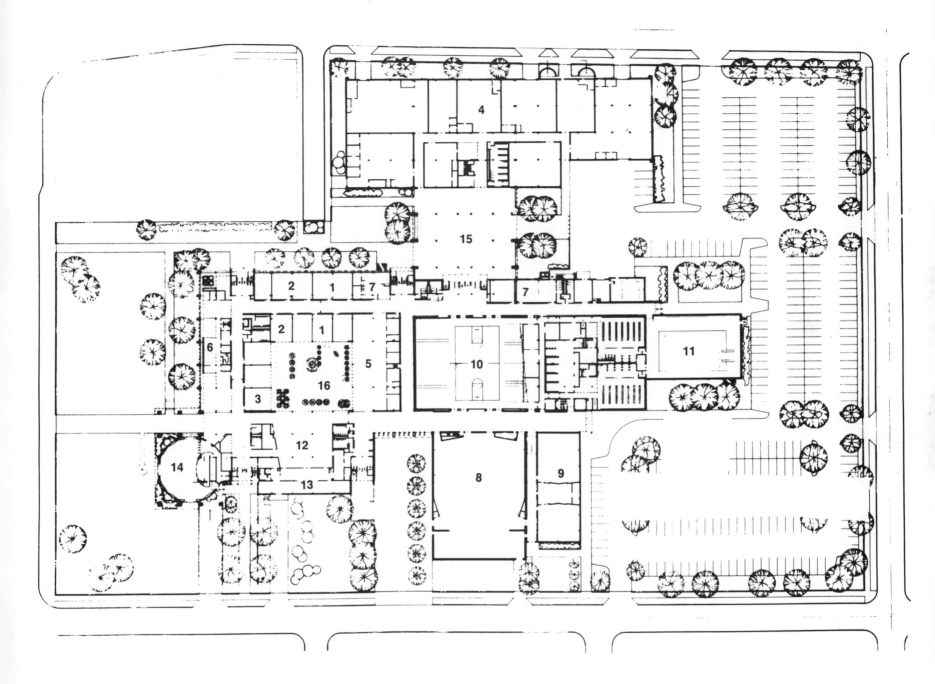

First floor plan - Site plan:

1 English classrooms
2 Social studies classrooms
3 Math classrooms
4 Vocational shops and classrooms
5 Sophomore library
6 Administration
7 Health
8 Auditorium

9 Music
10 Gymnasium
11 Swimming pool
12 Sophomore cafeteria
13 Kitchen
14 Group instruction and social room
15 Covered court
16 Court

Second floor plan:

1 English
2 Social studies
3 Math
4 Foreign language
5 Biology
6 Chemistry
7 Vocational business subjects
8 Art
9 Home economics
10 Junior library
11 Guidance
12 Auditorium, upper part
13 Gymnasium, upper part
14 Junior cafeteria

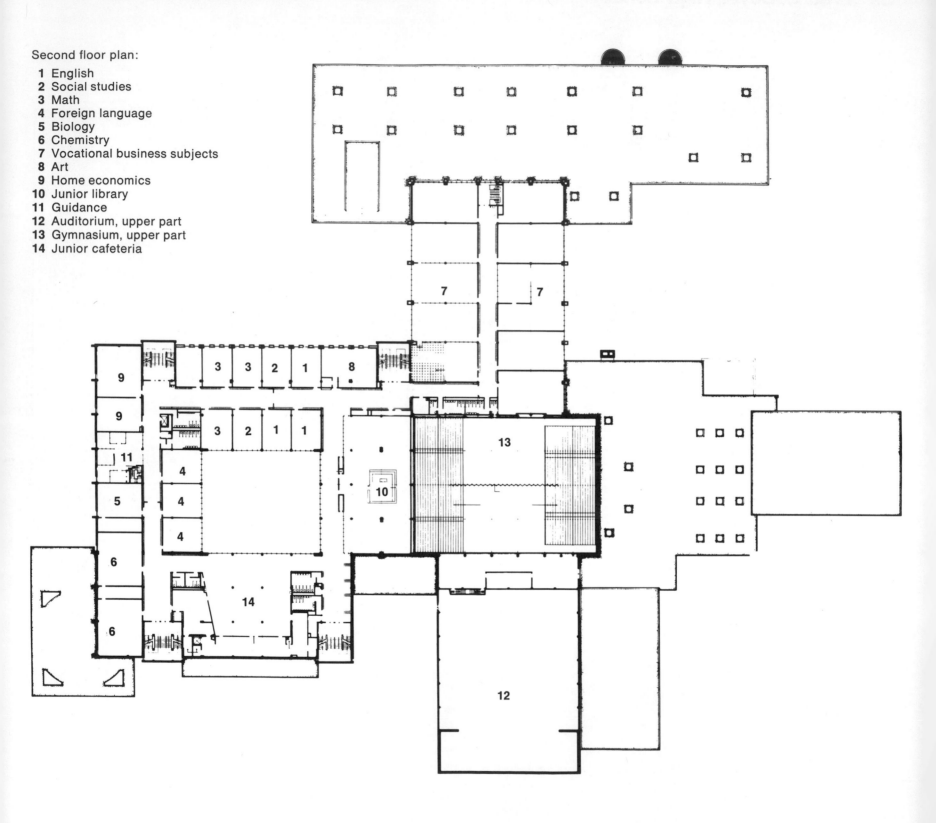

59 Fred C. Beyer High School

Owner Modesto City School District, Modesto, California

Superintendent Dr. Bert Corona

Architects Porter-Jensen & Associates, Santa Clara, California

Project architect George Babbit

Structural engineer Charles Uhrhammer

Electrical engineers David Arrigoni & Associates

Mechanical engineers George Greene Co.

Occupancy August 1972

Capacity 2,400

Organization 10-12

Construction costs $5,088,000

Demountable partitioning arranged honeycomb-fashion in all instructional areas was the architect's response to a program calling for every variation in teaching patterns — from the one-teacher, self-contained classroom technique to team teaching and flexible scheduling. The building is air conditioned and carpeted throughout.

Floor plan:
1 Large group instruction
2 Individual study area
3 English
4 Social studies
5 Foreign languages
6 Home economics
7 Business
8 Laboratories, science, math
9 Visual arts center
10 Industrial arts
11 Teacher preparation
12 Resource center
13 Sub-resource center
14 Administration
15 Performing arts
16 Forum, little theater, bandshell
17 Gymnasium
18 Pool
19 Showers and lockers
20 Food service
21 Student court
22 Science and agricultural court

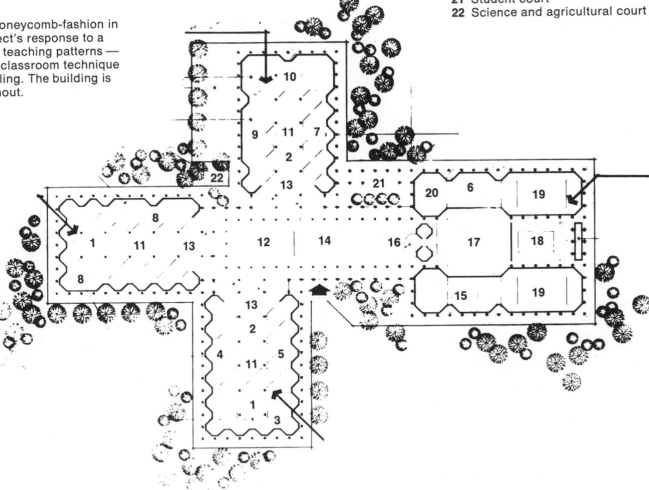

60 New Columbus High School

Owner Bartholomew Consolidated School Corporation, Columbus, Indiana

Superintendent Dr. Clarence E. Robbins

Principal Leroy Nelson

Architects Mitchell/Giurgola Associates, Philadelphia, Pennsylvania

Project architect Fred L. Foote

Structural engineers Keast & Hood Co.

Mechanical engineers Paul H. Yeomans, Inc.

Occupancy September 1972

Capacity 2,100

Organization 10-12

Project costs $14,115,000

Construction costs $11,344,000

In what might be called open planning on the diagonal, the architects here have designed a high school in which students will follow a flexible modular schedule. Under such schedules, students move independently from course to course or project to project, employing as many time modules — for example, 20-minute modules — as the course material or project requires. The school is an interesting addition to a community already nationally renowned for the quality of its public architecture.

Resource center:

1 English: teacher and student stations
2 Social studies: teacher and student stations
3 Foreign language: teacher and student stations
4 Mathematics: teacher and student stations
5 Science: Teacher and student stations
6 Business education: teacher and student stations
7 Art: teacher and student stations
8 Home economics: teacher and student stations
9 Instructional materials center

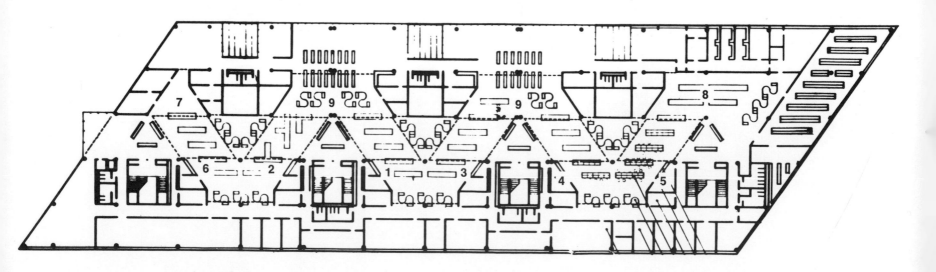

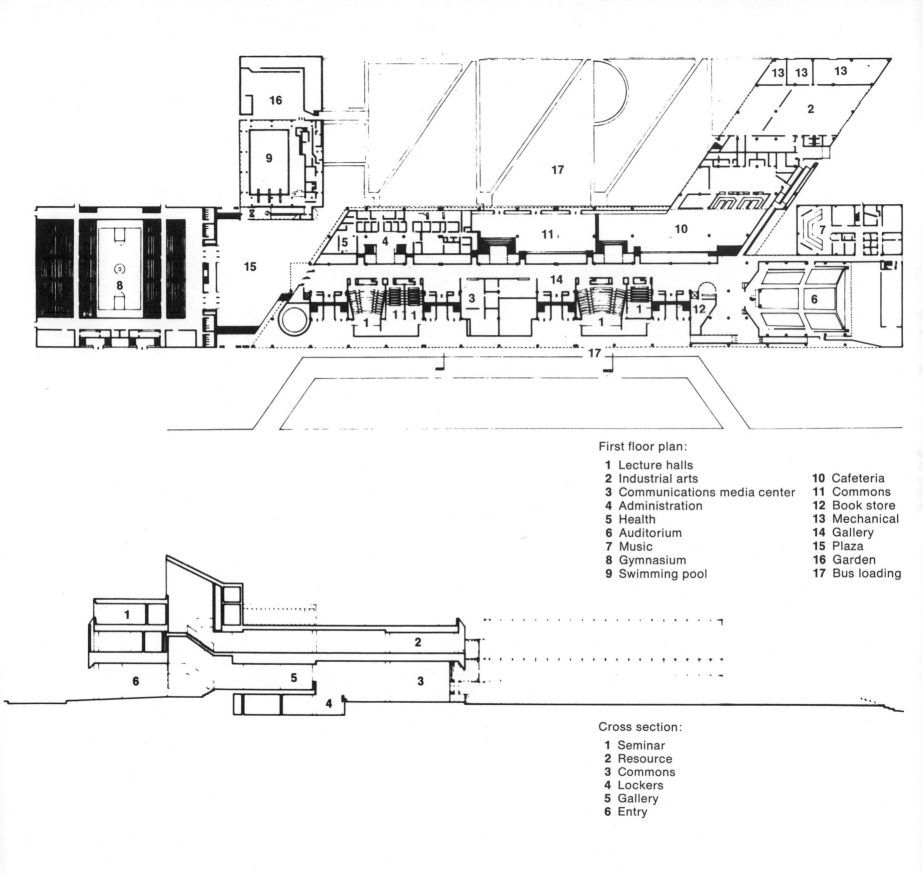

First floor plan:

1 Lecture halls
2 Industrial arts
3 Communications media center
4 Administration
5 Health
6 Auditorium
7 Music
8 Gymnasium
9 Swimming pool
10 Cafeteria
11 Commons
12 Book store
13 Mechanical
14 Gallery
15 Plaza
16 Garden
17 Bus loading

Cross section:

1 Seminar
2 Resource
3 Commons
4 Lockers
5 Gallery
6 Entry

61 Juanita High School

Owner Lake Washington School District, Juanita Beach, Washington

Superintendent Dr. Donald W. Empey

Principal John Strauss

Architects Kirk, Wallace, McKinley, AIA and Associates, Seattle, Washington

Project architect Keith Jacobson

Structural engineers Skillin, Helle, Christiansen, Robertson

Mechanical engineers Benjamin S. Notkin & Associates

Electrical engineers Sparling & Associates

Acoustical Robin Towne & Associates

Landscaping Richard Haag Associates, Inc.

Occupancy September 1971

Capacity 1,600

Organization 10-12

Project costs $5,593,861

Construction costs $4,533,839

In this rare application, the school-without-walls concept has been implemented in a high school. A huge, square, open area, 275 feet x 275 feet, totalling 63,690 square feet, will accommodate most of the school's instructional programs. Laboratories and spaces requiring acoustic isolation or privacy are located at the perimeter and partitioned off. Movable furniture and casework will be employed to define teaching spaces and provide visual privacy within the open area. The openness and flexibility of the area is made possible in part by a structural system in which columns are located 55 feet on center.

Floor plan:
1 Open area
2 Team teaching
3 Business education
4 Special purpose laboratories
5 Shops
6 Instructional materials
7 Administration
8 Performing arts
9 Little theater
10 Field house
11 Exercise gymnasium over lockers
12 Pool
13 Lockers
14 Kitchen
15 The Kiva
16 Parliament
17 Service system

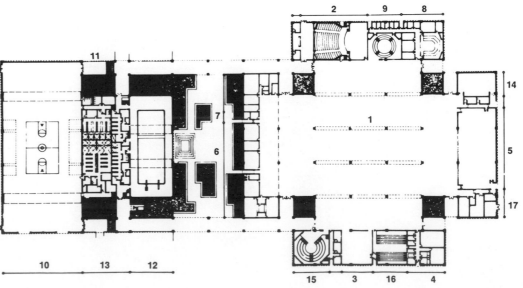

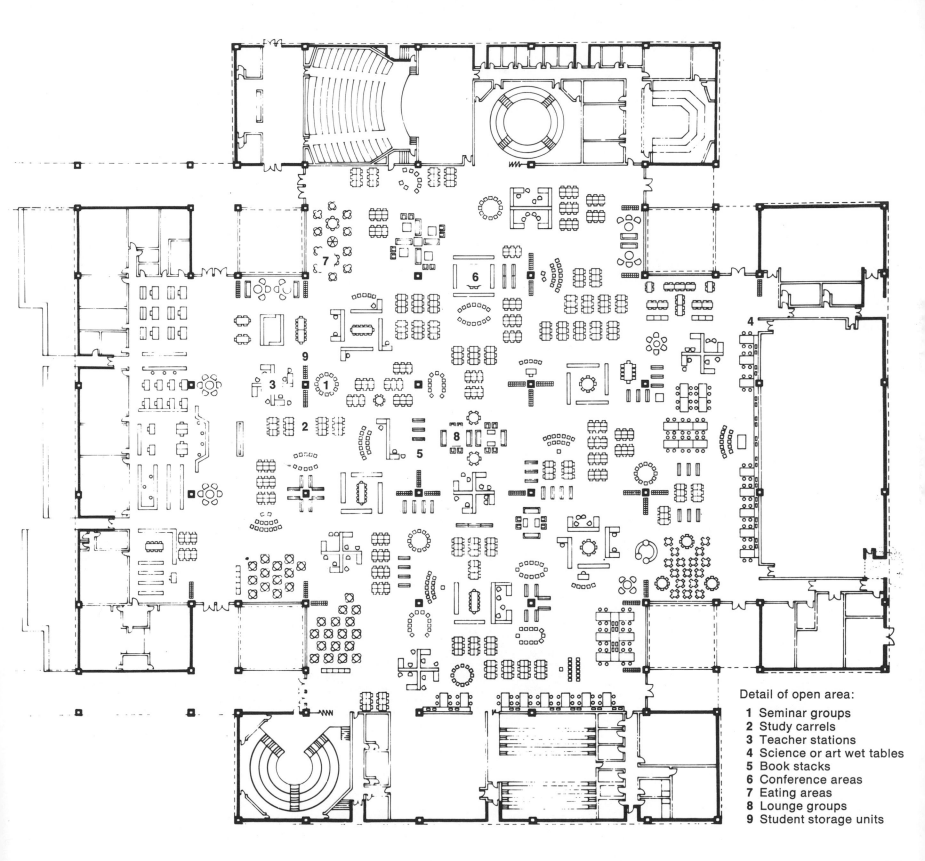

Detail of open area:

1 Seminar groups
2 Study carrels
3 Teacher stations
4 Science or art wet tables
5 Book stacks
6 Conference areas
7 Eating areas
8 Lounge groups
9 Student storage units

62 Anniston Educational Park

Owner Anniston City Board of Education, Anniston, Alabama

Superintendent Dr. George L. Layton

Associated architects Caudill Rowlett Scott, Houston/ New York/Hartford; Poole Pardue Morrison Deane, Birmingham, Alabama

Occupancy 1970 (first phase)

Capacity 1,100 (first phase), 3,620 (ultimate)

Organization Preschool-14

Project costs $2,518,100

The educational park, in which all elements of an educational system are combined on one site, drew wide attention in the 1960s as a possible tool for school integration, educational efficiency, and economy. One of the few communities to actually implement the idea was Anniston, Alabama, which plans a complex that eventually will house everything from preschool programs for three-year-olds to studies at the second-year level of college. Floor plans shown here are of the first phase, a high-school-level facility. Site plan for ultimate development shows educational facilities ranging from preschool (at right) to grades 13-14 (at left).

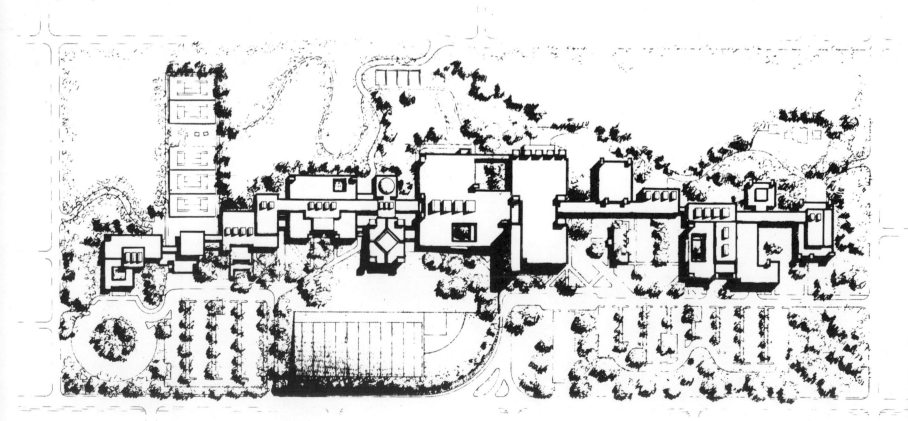

Site plan

First level floor plan:

1 Math-science area
2 Computers
3 Materials resource center
4 Materials resource sub-center
5 Administration
6 Auditorium
7 Gymnasium
8 Food service
9 Maintenance service
10 Lobby

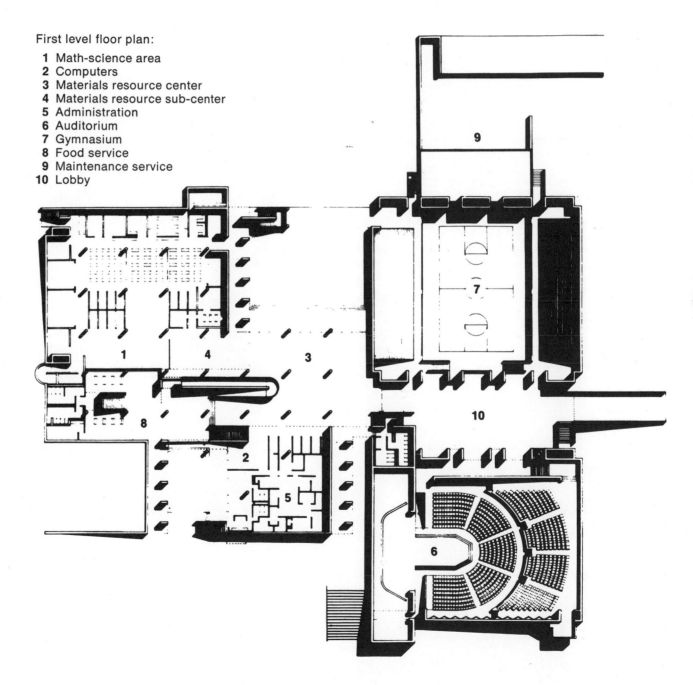

63 Julia S. Molloy Education Center

Owner Niles Township Department of Special Education, Niles, Illinois

Superintendent Dr. Vernon Frazee

Principal Julia S. Molloy

Architects Cone & Dornbusch, Chicago, Illinois

Mechanical engineers Kerekes & Kerekes

Structural engineers Samartano & Associates

Occupancy September 1970

Capacity 200

Organization Semi-graded

Project costs $935,000

Construction costs $780,247

There has been increasing attention in recent years to the problem of educating the trainable mentally retarded. In some areas, legislation has been adopted mandating such programs for the retarded up to age 21. The Julia S. Molloy Education Center is an example of a facility designed specifically for this purpose. Special features include close supervision of pupils and observation spaces for teacher trainees and visiting educators. Separate instructional areas are provided for three levels of mental ability: primary, intermediate, and accelerated.

Site plan:

1 Classroom unit
2 Music and art
3 Therapy area
4 Multi-use area
5 Amphitheater
6 Play area
7 Garage

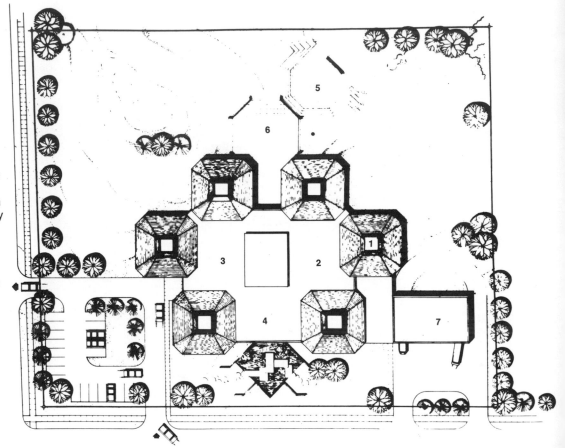

Longitudinal section:

1 Classroom unit
2 Music room
3 Therapy pool
4 Observation deck
5 Gymnasium
6 Faculty lounge
7 Mechanical space
8 Structural members

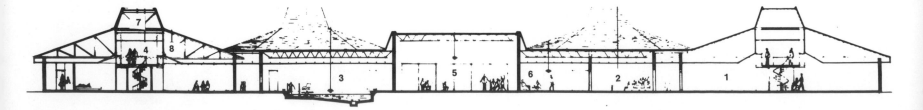

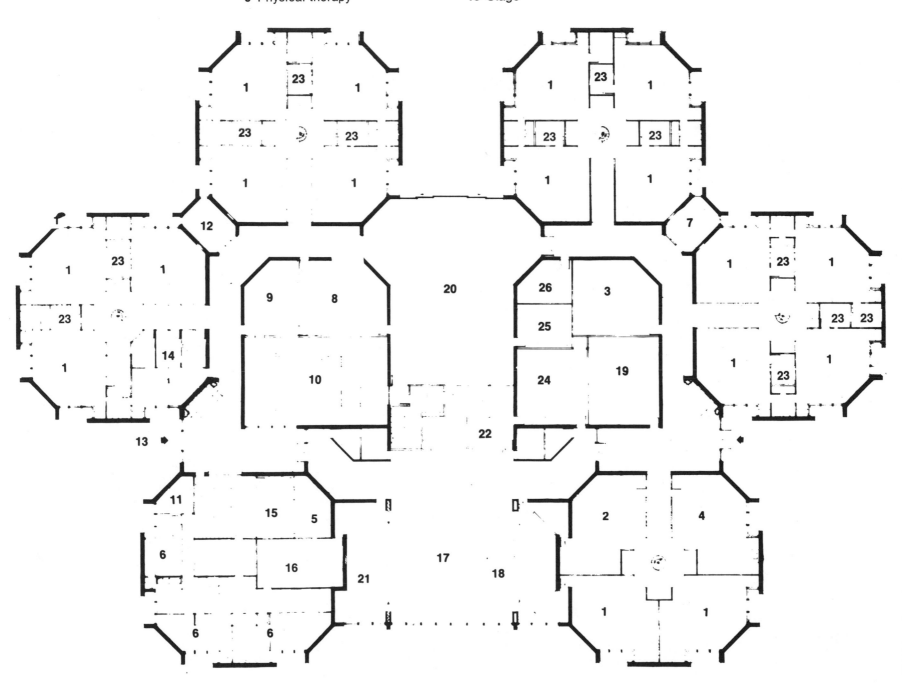

Floor plan:

1 Classroom	10 Therapy tank	19 Music
2 Learning laboratory	11 Social worker	20 Gymnasium
3 Arts and crafts	12 Waiting	21 Faculty and volunteers' dining
4 Home-making	13 Visitors	22 Kitchen
5 Library	14 Health and social work facilities	23 Time-out room
6 Administration	15 Conference and reading room	24 Faculty lounge
7 Faculty conference and workroom	16 Conference room	25 Mechanical
8 Occupational therapy·	17 Multi-use area	26 Storage
9 Physical therapy	18 Stage	

64 Wiltwyck School for Boys

Owner Wiltwyck School for Boys, Inc., Yorktown, New York

Principal Joseph Wynne

Architects Richard G. Stein and Associates, New York, New York

Structural engineers Fraioli, Blum, Yesselman

Mechanical engineers S. A. Bogen Engineers

Acoustical Michael J. Kodaras, Inc.

Estimating McKee-Berger-Mansueto, Inc.

Food service John C. Mason

Graphics Appelbaum & Curtis

Specifications Leon A. Langner

Occupancy September 1966

Capacity 100

Organization non-graded

Construction costs $3,418,040

This school, a residential treatment center, was designed to provide living, educational, therapeutic, and recreational facilities for 100 emotionally disturbed, pre-adolescent boys. Different functions are housed in separate buildings on the 109-acre, hilly and rocky campus.

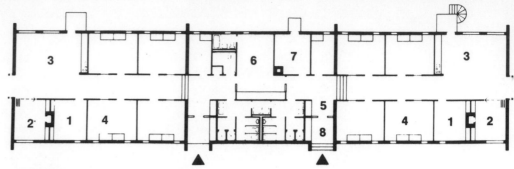

Children's residence building
First floor plan:

1 Study
2 Living room
3 Playroom
4 Bedroom
5 Mud room
6 Staff and night counselor
7 Boiler
8 Entry

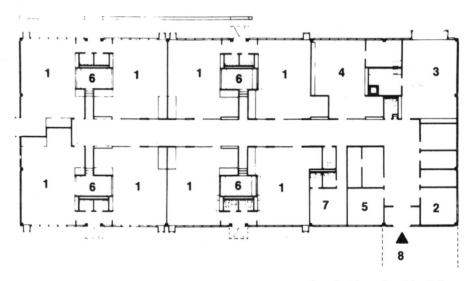

Academic school building
First floor plan:

1 Classroom
2 Remedial
3 Science room
4 Library
5 Principal's office
6 Observation room
7 Teachers' room
8 Covered link

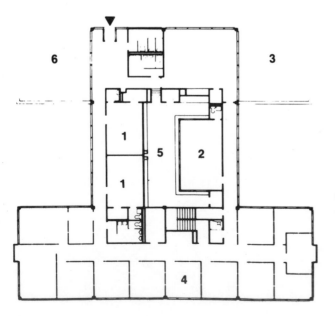

Clinical and research building
Second floor plan:

1 Group therapy
2 Play therapy
3 Library - lecture room
4 Offices
5 Observation and audio-visual control
6 Entry and waiting

Site plan:

1 Academic school building
2 Administration building
3 Child care administration building
4 Medical and dental building
5 Clinical and research building
6 Activities building
7 Gymnasium building
8 Dining and activities building
9 Children's residence building
10 Staff apartments
11 Garage and staff quarters
12 Storage
13 Storage and issue building
14 Garage and storage

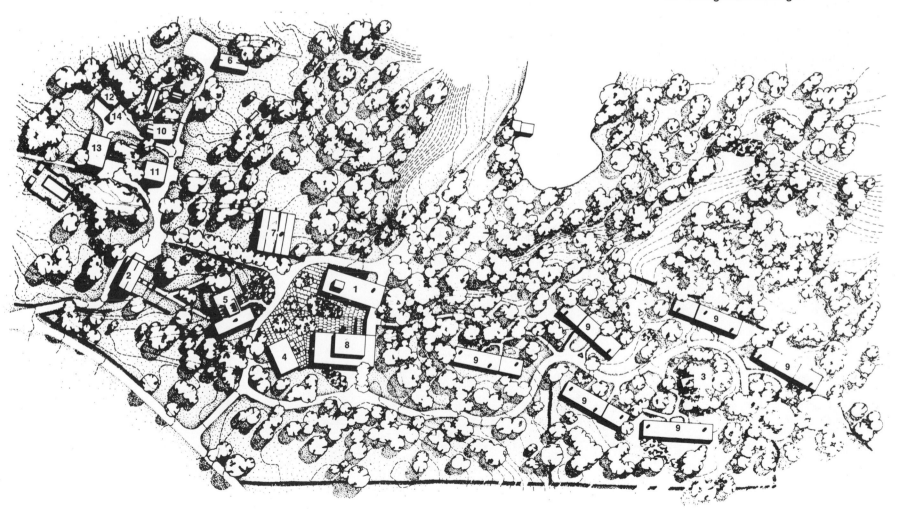

65 Palm Avenue Exceptional Child Center (Public School 170), Jacksonville, Florida

Owner Duval County School Board, Florida

Superintendent Dr. Cecil D. Hardesty

Program coordinator Mrs. Phyllis M. Zando

Architect William Morgan, Jacksonville, Florida

Project architect John Dyal

Structural engineer Haley W. Keister

Mechanical-electrical engineers Evans & Hammond, Inc.

Occupancy January 1971

Capacity 150

Organization non-graded, ages 6-16

Project costs $460,725

Construction costs $367,100

Five pavilions of residential rather than institutional scale comprise this school for the trainable mentally retarded. In the instructional pavilions, operable partitions close off four classrooms from a central, skylighted assembly area, allowing for a variety of instructional groupings. Sliding chalkboards give access to outdoor teaching terraces and play areas.

Floor plan:

1 Primary classrooms
2 Intermediate classrooms
3 Advanced grades: 13, 14, 15
4 Pre-occupation
5 Shop
6 Audio-visual laboratories
7 Family living
8 Administration
9 Clerical
10 Meeting
11 Therapy pool
12 Assembly
13 Kitchen
14 Apartment
15 Equipment

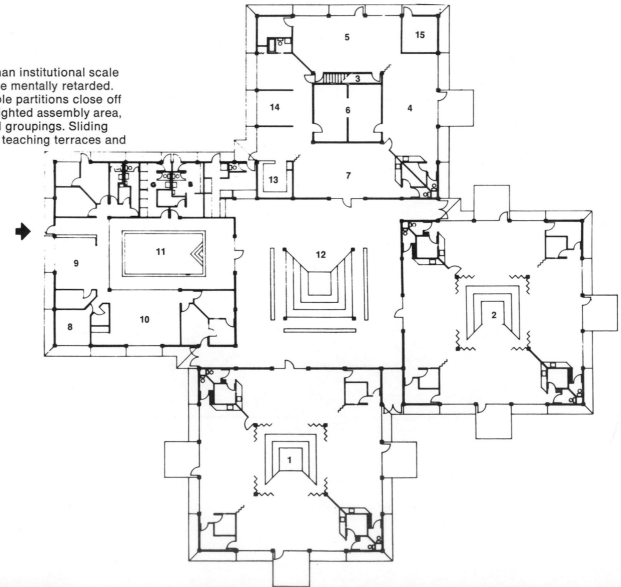

Other Van Nostrand Reinhold Books for Architects and Planners

Exterior Design in Architecture
Yoshinobu Ashihara
A handbook for architects on the theory and practice of designing exterior space: the exterior of buildings, the setting for groups of buildings, city plazas, gardens, etc. 144 pages, 10 x 10, handsomely illustrated.

Pencil Techniques in Modern Design
William W. Atkin and others
Presents a wide variety of pencil techniques suitable for renderings and presentation drawings: fine line, pencil painting, scumbling, broad stroke, bold line. 128 pages, $9^{1}/_8$ x $12^{1}/_4$, 250 illustrations.

Architectural Presentation in Opaque Watercolor: Theory and Technique
Chris Choate
"Altogether, this book is tops — a must for anyone interested in a new technique . . ." — *Progressive Architecture.* 160 pages, $8^{3}/_4$ x $10^{1}/_2$, 200 illustrations.

Architecture: Action and Plan
Peter Cook
A study of architecture and the elements that compose it: space, sequence, scale, siting. Rewarding reading for any serious student of architecture. 96 pages, $6^{1}/_2$ x $7^{3}/_4$, 125 illustrations; paperback.

Step-by-Step Perspective Drawing
Claudius Coulin
A guide that enables the architect, draftsman, or designer to teach himself more about technical drawing than is taught in many drafting schools. Also valuable for reference and review. 112 pages, $8^{1}/_2$ x 11, 43 pages of drawings.

The Concise Townscape
Gordon Cullen
The paperback version of Cullen's *Townscape,* which is the classic study of the visual elements of town planning. 192 pages, 6 x 8, 200 illustrations.

Contemporary Houses: Evaluated by Their Owners
Thomas Hawk Creighton
Thirty-six owners of custom-designed houses tell what they like and what they don't like about their houses. Valuable both to architects and to anyone planning to build. 224 pages, $8^{1}/_8$ x $10^{1}/_2$, 209 illustrations.

Design for Play
Richard Dattner
New approaches to the urban playground, with many photographs and drawings. 144 pages, 11 x $8^{1}/_2$ (oblong).

Cities
Lawrence Halprin
An original study of the environmental needs of people, as expressed by city layout and public spaces in old and new cities here and abroad. 224 pages, $10^{1}/_4$ x $8^{1}/_4$ (oblong), 400 illustrations.

Freeways
Lawrence Halprin
The author finds beauty as well as function in freeways, as long as they are well designed and properly adapted to the natural and man-made environment. 160 pages, $10^{1}/_4$ x $8^{1}/_4$ (oblong), 279 illustrations.

Architectural and Interior Models
Sanford Hohauser
How to plan, estimate, construct, and photograph models, with dozens of lists of tools and materials and hundreds of photographs and drawings. 224 pages, 9 x 12, 400 illustrations.

Drawing as a Means to Architecture
William Kirby Lockard
A method of using graphic techniques very early in the design process, as an inseparable part of architectural planning rather than merely as a method of communication. 96 pages, 12 x 9 (oblong), 50 illustrations.

A House in the City
H. Dickson McKenna
A guide to buying and renovating nineteenth-century row houses, with hundreds of photographs, line drawings, and plans. Written by an architect for the layman. 160 pages, $8^{1}/_2$ x 11, 250 illustrations.

Ships and Boats: The Nature of Their Design
Douglas Phillips-Birt
A thoughtful study of the elements of naval architecture. 96 pages, $7^{3}/_4$ x $6^{1}/_2$, 64 illustrations; available hardbound or paperback.

New Movement in Cities
Brian Richards
Suggestions on how to solve the problems of public transportation. 96 pages, $7^{3}/_4$ x $6^{1}/_2$, 147 illustrations; paperback.

Modern American Gardens
James C. Rose
Examples of the author's imaginative approach to landscape architecture. 224 pages, 9 x 12, 300 illustrations.

How to Use Creative Perspective
Ernest W. Watson
A helpful guide for architects and others who are occasionally required to draw in perspective. 160 pages, $8^1/_4$ x $10^3/_8$, 350 illustrations.

Perspective for Sketchers
Ernest W. Watson
How to utilize drafting principles in freehand techniques. 48 pages, $7^3/_4$ x $10^1/_2$, illustrated.

Architecture: A Book of Projects for Young Adults
Forrest Wilson
Provides the young person who is interested in architecture with a basic understanding of architectural and engineering principles, and encourages his interest. 96 pages, 8 x 8, 200 illustrations.

Architecture and Interior Environment: A Book of Projects for Young Adults
Forrest Wilson
A stimulating discussion of the natural and mechanical means man has found to control his environment, from cave to space capsule. 96 pages, 8 x 8, 200 illustrations.

Structure: The Essence of Architecture
Forrest Wilson
Explains how man has mastered the art of building, and how he must learn to master his built environment. 96 pages, $6^1/_2$ x $7^3/_4$, 200 illustrations; available hardbound or paperback.

Trees for Architecture and the Landscape
Robert L. Zion
An explanation of both the architectural and the horticultural considerations of landscape design, with winter and summer portraits of many species. 284 pages, 9 x 12, many illustrations.